WALT IN WONDERLAND
THE SILENT FILMS OF WALT DISNEY

Russell Merritt
J.B. Kaufman

WALT
in Wonderland

**The Silent Films
of Walt Disney**

LE GIORNATE
DEL CINEMA
MUTO

Distributed by
The Johns Hopkins University Press

This is a revised, English language edition of the bilingual volume *Nel paese delle meraviglie: i cartoni animati muti di Walt Disney / Walt in Wonderland: The Silent Films of Walt Disney* published in 1992 by Le Giornate del Cinema Muto, Pordenone, Italy, in cooperation with Edizioni Biblioteca dell'Immagine and with support of Regione Friuli-Venezia Giulia, Comune di Pordenone, Provincia di Pordenone, Ministero del Turismo e dello Spettacolo.

Copyright © 1993 by Russell Merritt / J.B. Kaufman
Le Giornate del Cinema Muto / La Cineteca del Friuli
ISBN 88-86155-02-6

Cover by Giulio Calderini
Mickey Mouse copyright © The Walt Disney Company

Distributed by
The Johns Hopkins University Press
2715 North Charles Street
Baltimore, Maryland 21218-4319
ISBN 0-8018-4907-1

CONTENTS

INTRODUCTION

There is probably no other figure in modern popular culture connected with as many different images and associations as Walt Disney. Some regard him as an original American genius, a master storyteller who through his animated films had a revolutionary effect on the folklore of the world. Others see him as the avuncular Horatio Alger, a midwestern go-getter who catered to American mid-cult values with his love of the cute, the sentimental, and the familiar. Still others see him as a megalomaniac whose TV series and amusement parks form a vital part of American cultural imperialism.

But all these Walt Disneys — public figure, entertainer, entrepreneur, artist — find their origins in a single source: the ambitious young man who struggled to establish his first animation studio in the 1920s. Of this Walt Disney surprisingly little is known. Books on his career and artistic achievements tend to gloss over his work in silent films, strongly implying that that work was of no importance. The Alice and Oswald the Lucky Rabbit films that Disney produced during those years rarely rate more than a cursory mention. The result is that the first eight years of Disney's film career have been virtually ignored or, when described, riddled with misinformation.

This book is the story of those eight years, and of the films Disney and his collaborators produced. We have divided our text into two unequal parts. Our first section provides a critical overview of Disney's work during this period, a kind of free-form speculation on the most important qualities of Disney's silent work. In the second, longer section, we revert to a detailed historical account of Disney's studio activities. Here we set forth a large body of previously uncollated information within the context of the Disney studio's economic and artistic development. Drawing from business papers, promotional materials, scripts, drawings, and correspondence, we chronicle what is known about his silent film career.

We have interviewed survivors too, most importantly Virginia Davis McGhee, Rudy Ising, Friz Freleng, Anne Shirley Lederer, Marjorie Sewell Davis, Ruthie Tompson, and Dr. John Records. Our thanks go to all of them for their patience and generosity in sharing their recollections with us.

Disney's silent films, hidden for so long in the shadow of Disney's later accomplishments — many of them literally hidden in remote archives and private collections — flesh out our image of Disney the artist. They show him taking his first tentative steps, then gathering confidence and exploring new avenues of expression, in images that are still fresh and exhilarating today. They bear out the intuition of common sense: that Mickey Mouse was not created in a vacuum, and that Disney was developing and focusing his gifts as a producer from the beginning.

In the course of it all, we have been obliged to discard several preconceived notions, particularly in regards to Disney's development as an animation director/producer.

We were surprised to find, for instance, that many — perhaps most — of the famous gags and routines in the 1930s Disney were already part of his comic vocabulary by the end of the 1920s. The Laugh-O-grams, Alices, and Oswalds were among other things rough drafts for many of the Silly Symphonies and Mickey Mouse cartoons. One consequence is that an overlay of silent film conventions enfold Disney's 1930s and early 1940s animation long after rival live-action producers had abandoned them. For all the advances Disney makes in animation techniques, his ideas about acting in cartoons, scene staging, lighting, and narrative structure are firmly entrenched in the silents of the 1920s.

Contrariwise, many conventions of animation lore, familiar from the 1930s on, had not yet been developed in Disney's silent period. The concept of "squash and stretch," the underlying principle of Disney's fluid animation style, is taken for granted today — but we can see it evolving, hesitantly, through trial and error, in the silent films. The technique of cel animation, a standard procedure by the time of Mickey Mouse, likewise develops in experimental fashion throughout the silent period. To re-examine the road Disney took to evolve these techniques is to see all of Disney's animated films in a fresh light.

A spelling note. To the modern animation enthusiast, the man known as "Ub Iwerks" needs no introduction. But the original spelling of the artist's given name was Ubbe Ert Iwwerks, and throughout the 1920s his first name was rendered "Ubbe" in Disney studio records. It is, therefore, so rendered in this book. Similarly the man familiar to later generations as "Rudolf Ising" was still spelling his first name "Rudolph" in the silent period, and we have retained that spelling in these pages. On the other hand, even though animations cels were invariably called "cells" in the 1920s, in this instance we caved in and used the modern spelling.

And one identification note. Amidst our research, we were startled to learn of the existence of an uncredited Alice who over the years had been turned into a non-person. The last ten films attributed to Margie Gay in fact starred someone else, a young girl who was several years older than Margie and a far more expressive actress. Disney in fact called her "the best Alice yet." Through the detective work we describe in the Alice chapter we have been able to identify this charming youngster as Lois Hardwick.

We have been benefitted from the generous cooperation of many people and organizations. At the Walt Disney Company, we are especially grateful to Howard Green, director of studio communications, who was instrumental in gaining for us the studio's active cooperation. The Walt Disney Archives, headed by David R. Smith, provided indispensible material and showed us their customary hospitality and patience. The Disney brothers had a strong sense of history, and even in this early obscure period their care in preserving their records has been invaluable for the historian. Special thanks to the extraordinary Disney archival staff — Robert Tieman, Jennie Hendrickson, and Rose Motzko.

The authors viewed Disney films both at the Disney archives and at other major archives in the United States. Warm thanks are due to Jere Guldin at the UCLA film archive, and Charles Silver and his Film Study Center staff at the Museum of Modern Art. We also thank Richard Koszarski at the American Museum of the Moving Image for sharing his expertise and his private collection of Universal materials. The Library of Congress holds the largest public collection of Disney silents in the United States, and we are especially indebted to Madeline Matz, the Library's film and television research librarian, who took time from a hectic schedule and went far beyond the call of duty with her generous assistance. Among private collectors, Virginia McGhee, Bob Birchard, David Shepard and Jan Wahl were particularly generous in sharing films, rare books and valuable insights. Mike Barrier made significant contributions, particularly in sharing relevant sections of an interview with Carman Maxwell. For his technical expertise we are indebted to George Turner, editor emeritus of *American Cinematographer*. And for their kind hospitality, we owe a debt of thanks to Barbara Moser Schaible in Maryland, and to Howard and Gail Prouty in California.

In Europe, we gratefully acknowledge the help of Mark-Paul Meyer of the Nederlands Filmmuseum, whose archive is second only to the Disney company itself in the scope and quality of its silent Disney collection. We also thank collector David Wyatt in London for sharing his collection and research.

This book was originally written in conjunction with a retrospective of Disney's silent films held by the Giornate del Cinema Muto in Pordenone, Italy in October 1992. The Giornate provided the first comprehensive review of Disney's silent work. With its customary thoroughness, it screened virtually all known survivors — some fifty-eight shorts out of the approximately one hundred he produced.

The Giornate originally published a bilingual version of this book — our English text supplemented by an Italian translation. The present edition is English only, but all the original illustrations are here, plus several additional photos. No less than the original edition, this one is indebted to the Giornate's directorate. Without its material and moral support, many of the films discussed here, hidden in little-known European collections, would never have been published.

We were particularly fortunate to have for our editor Piera Patat, *la fata dai capelli turchini* for would-be historians. Her encouragement and sensitive contributions made this project a joy. For all his help with our original manuscript, we are grateful to Carlo Montanaro. We also thank the president of the Giornate del Cinema Muto and head of La Cineteca del Friuli, Livio Jacob, whose personal interest and commitment to quality publishing made us work all the harder. And, lastly, we thank Paolo Cherchi Usai for cooking up the book's snappy title.

DISNEY'S CAT AND RABBIT YEARS

It is hard to look at Disney's work in silent animation apart from the blinding afterimage of Mickey Mouse, the Silly Symphonies, and Disney's subsequent productions. Inevitably, the associations with Disney, the reinventor of fairy tales and amusement parks, the ubiquitous purveyor of American sweetness and light, affect what we look for when we watch his earliest films. Where did it all come from? Where are the clues that reveal Mickey and Snow White lurking in the wings? Were those bourgeois values always there, lurking below the surface like some Faustian devil, or did they only come later with prosperity and creeping middle age?

And even if we could get past these questions and associations, we are confronted with another impulse equally compelling: the determination to find forward directions, straightline evolutions within his 1920s work. We want to see growth from the crude to the complex. What are the breakthroughs? Where are the landmarks? Where and when were the seeds for sophisticated narrative planted? How did they grow?

And yet the first striking fact about Disney's 1920s films is that they take no particular direction: they don't evolve, they accumulate. What we would expect from a director as aggressive and driven as Disney is a series of films that would build exponentially, one upon the other, somewhat in the manner of the Griffith Biographs or the Chaplin Mutuals. Yet something rather different occurs. In many ways, Disney's first films in Kansas City seem as accomplished as his later Hollywood silents. We have to wait for several years to find a film as well-paced, as thematically rich, or with backgrounds as provocative and well-drawn as his earliest surviving Laugh-O-gram fairy tales such as *Little Red Riding Hood*, *Puss in Boots*, and *Cinderella*. His lead cartoon character in his series of Alice animated comedies, Julius the cat, does not evolve from derivative cliche to a fresh, original character. On the contrary, he retreats in the opposite direction, growing more imitative of Otto Messmer's Felix the Cat as he goes along. If one can describe a general tendency in the Alice backgrounds (albeit with important exceptions) it is towards cruder, sketchier, and more innocuous landscapes. The rich, signifying background details in films like *Alice's Egg Plant*, *Alice Picks the Champ*, and *Alice Rattled by Rats* precede rather than follow the crude stickwork in *Alice the Fire Fighter* and *Alice's Brown Derby*, and his Oswald the Lucky Rabbit films like *Trolley Troubles* and *The Mechanical Cow*. Symptomatically, Disney traded the talented Virginia Davis for the pedestrian Margie Gay to play Alice, so that the promising and frequently charming interactions between Alice and Julius soon deteriorate into Alice's pro-forma live-action appearances with Alice doing little more than flapping her arms. For about a year Disney developed the rich possibilities of a comic partnership between a little girl and an animated playmate, but he then appears to have lost interest, turning Julius into a Felix copycat and Alice into a passive observer.

In short, anyone expecting an endless succession of experimentation, rule-bending, and dazzling breakthroughs is doomed to disappointment. As early as 1925, Disney was already remaking earlier films and recycling gags. When Disney found a joke or comic routine that was successful, he hung onto it tenaciously, and working to deliver one cartoon per month, he constantly repeated himself. The overall impression is of a talented craftsman working safely within the prescribed limits of comic animation defined by others — particularly the producers of Felix the Cat, Koko the Clown, and Krazy Kat. The Alices and the Oswalds are in every way apprentice films, witty and frequently charming, providing Disney with a storehouse of gags, plot ideas, and secondary characters that he could reintroduce and refine in his 1930s shorts. What the silent Disneys principally document is Disney's training as a mainstream animation director, mining the same graphic, comic, and narrative sources that also served his more illustrious contemporaries.

The story of Disney's silent film career is not so much a struggle for artistic expression as it is a fight for commercial stability. Disney started his animation career in 1920 as a commercial artist working for an advertising company, producing promotional fillers that were exhibited in local theaters. In the years that followed, he plied his not entirely reputable trade in some of the toughest neighborhoods within the film industry: the law-of-the-jungle independent trade where speed, alertness, and adaptability were essential skills. Over and again he is fleeced — first in Kansas City where he set up his Laugh-O-gram studio in 1922 and 1923 and then was driven bankrupt, then with his Alice Comedies which he made in Hollywood between 1924 and 1927, and finally with his Oswald cartoons produced in 1927 and 1928, where he lost his rabbit hero to his bare-knuckled distributor. If there is a simple theme or thread in these years, it is an economic one — Disney's determination to become a successful independent entrepreneur, beholden to no one.

In this atmosphere, it is unsurprising that Disney worked diligently within the confines of popular 1920s cartoon formulas. What is remarkable is that Disney's work also reveals virtually from the beginning strategies and motifs that become identifying signatures. And if throughout the 1920s his animation stays limited to match stick figures with rubber hose limbs, we can find perceptible experiments with screen personality and staging that keep shooting through. Disney gags are intrinsically no better than other studios' but they were frequently organized with greater skill, with particular concern for detail, and as Disney matures, a concern for building comic routines, for making gags pay off. As Ben Sharpsteen said, "I think that Walt was initially inspired by animation that stressed personality. The strong impression that it made on him led to his desire to plug it in subsequent pictures."[1]

Disney the mythologizer still lay far in the future. The silent filmmaker shows no predilection for symbol and myth, or for that matter even much nostalgia. The closest he gets to monumentalizing the past is in his affectionate lampoons of Victorian melodrama in his first Alices — the restaging of Eliza's pursuit by Simon Legree in *Alice Stage Struck* or strapping Alice to a log leading to a buzz saw in *Alice and the Three Bears*. But his eye is plainly on the fast-moving, unpretentious string of gags uncomplicated by mythic resonance. The nursery literature recycled in his earliest surviving films at Laugh-O-gram — *Puss in Boots*, *The Four Musicians of Bremen*, *Little Red Riding Hood*, and *Cinderella* — is little more than a starting point for conventional chase gags. In fact, Disney had to fight for what little narrative development his Alices and Oswalds do show.

Over and again his distributors insist that he concentrate on packing his films with more and more gags, and not get bogged down in plot development. The response to his first Hollywood film is characteristic. On January 9, 1924, Margaret Winkler wires him about *Alice's Day at Sea*, "Not all that I expected it to be ... I would suggest you inject as much humor as you possibly can. Humor is the first requisite of short subjects such as Felix, Out of the Inkwell, and Alice." About his next film, *Alice Hunting in Africa*, she remarks: "[Everybody] says that the subject is nice and clean and they like Alice very much but the lack of humor hurts sales." Disney dutifully toes the line. About *Alice and the Three Bears* he replies, "I am happy to say that it received as many laughs as the Felix, and at the same time, I feel we did not have as many laughs as some of our previous ones .... We are now making *Alice the Piper*; working for more laughs, leaving out little details of the story and putting in funny gags." About *Alice the Toreador* he explains why he preferred cartoon animals to live-action kids: "Animals afford bigger opportunity for laughs than people." Winkler's brother sums it up in a friendly letter to Walt: "Remember!! Bigger and Better Pictures, more grotesque, and full of Guffaws!" Then, when Charles Mintz, Winkler's husband and Disney's new distributor, threatens to reject *Alice Chops the Suey*, it is because "it has too much story and lacks in gags."[2] Mintz' idea of a great cartoon is the anemic *Alice the Fire Fighter*, nothing more than a string of old slapstick circus routines, but in Mintz's judgment "as good as anything you have turned out, snappy and funny." Only when he invents Oswald does he begin to test the water with the atmospherics of a bygone America. 1927 Oswalds such as *The Ole' Swimmin' Ole* and *Oh Teacher*, playing off the popularity of the Gus Edwards "School Days" vaudeville routines and Charles Ray comedies, insert individual shots to invoke America's nostalgic past. In *Neck 'n' Neck* he creates the first of many comic "buggy rides" featuring playful sweethearts out for a spin. But the requirements of rapid fire slapstick cut short any attempt to develop leisurely moods. The tyranny of the gag sharply restricted narrative development and characterization.

And yet (to return to one of the pleasures we started cautioning against), as bound by economic pressures and audience expectations as these cartoons were, they are saturated with what would become Disney's signature motifs. Pieced together, they form a cluster of themes that would develop and dominate his classic work of the thirties.

Above all was his effort to combine the unpretentious charm of the midwestern farm with his love of royalty, pageantry, and strict social hierarchy. As has been frequently noted, Disney's background as a farm boy working with animals developed into a broad range of films set in the countryside dominated by comic animals and a child-like entrepreneur. But what has been less frequently noticed is that this portrait of barnyard life was almost invariably intertwined with an equally persistent portrait of a kingdom, replete with a royal family, royal parades, and the storybook paraphernalia of court life. These incongruous forces that would merge with such commercial success in Disneyland mix and mingle in bizarre ways in even his earliest work. In *Alice the Piper*, the King of Hamlin is a farmer who sleeps in a farmhouse plagued by inventive mice. In *Puss in Boots* the local king lives in an authentic palace (or at least a mansion) incongruously set in the middle of a village with a main street and silent movie theater.

The blending of the royal kingdom with American small-town life. The midwestern king approaches his midwestern castle in *Puss in Boots*, while in downtown Kingville, the boy and his cat go the movies.

In this regard it doesn't much matter whether Alice and Oswald travel abroad, stay at home, or move into the past. When in *Alice's Wonderland*, Alice dreams herself into a fantasy village, the town residents greet her with a royal parade that culminates in a festival, with Alice as the guest of honor. When she is shipwrecked at the bottom of the sea in *Alice's Day at Sea* she encounters the creatures in "King Nep's Zoo" in a sequence that combines features of the royal court and the American circus. In the assorted films that bring Alice and Oswald in contact with the jungle and various cannibal tribes, an important part of the humor (such as it is) is the incongruity between the African cartoon court and the predilection for middle American comforts (the king who goes bowling or entertains himself with a radio).

Even when detached from the royal court, a Disney silent is seldom far removed from a world marked by a pageant of some sort, cheering on-lookers, a rigid social hierarchy, with an imperious (and invariably comic) authority figure. One common configuration is the arena sports event (such as the bull fight in *Alice the Toreador*, the baseball game in *Alice in the Big League*, the rodeo in *Alice's Rodeo* and *Alice's Wild West Show*, and the steeplechase in *Alice's Brown Derby*) where audiences flock to a stadium festooned with banners and pennants and applaud a knightly procession of buffoonish athlete heroes. Another is the secret cabal, the colorful outlaw organization with rituals and passwords with a set piece in which the gang members pay comic fealty to their outlaw chief who usually sits on a throne of some sort (*Alice and the Dog Catcher*, *Alice Foils the Pirates*, and *Alice's Mysterious Mystery* provide ready illustration).

Yet it is wrong to think that in this peaceable kingdom, where animals frolic and kings rule, Disney is soft on authority. On the contrary, Disney's sympathies are generally with those who goof off or tear the community apart. Authority figures are invariably absurd, and in the case of dog catchers and school teachers, heavily satiric. Disney fathers — invariably cartoon Pantaloons — exist to be outwitted. The Disney policeman — a cross between Offissa Pupp and a Keystone Kop — is the overworked, harassed spoilsport who's usually fighting a lost cause.

Krazy Kat: 25 April 1920 (left); 6 October 1940 (above).

The most common expression of irresponsibility is the lively dance: an unauthorized musical free-for-all or jamboree where underlings play hookey or overturn the conventional order. Film historian William Paul wrote in his penetrating article about music and *Pinocchio*, "From its beginnings, film has had a natural affinity for music

Alice Gets in Dutch: Disney lampoons authority in the live action frame featuring Mrs. Hunt (teacher), Virginia Davis, and Spec O'Donnell; bottom: teacher and her books as militaristic kill-joys. (Courtesy Virginia Davis McGhee) Overleaf: The characters in George Herriman's *Krazy Kat* were a formative influence on Disney, particularly in such films as *Alice the Peacemaker* and *The Banker's Daughter*. Compare Disney's "Pillicemin" and Herriman's Offissa Pupp. (Courtesy Walt Disney Company)

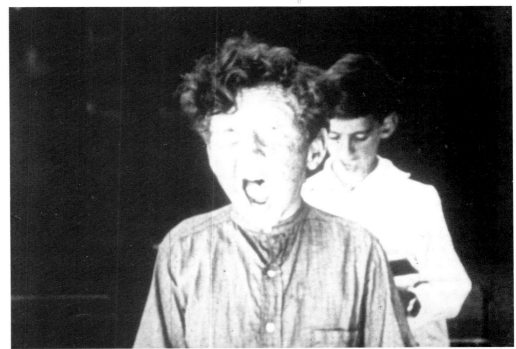

since both are art forms that move through time, but with cartoons this affinity is more like symbiosis. It was inevitable that a perfect rhythmic synchronization of music and movement, "mickey mousing," the closest possible marriage of sound and image, should draw on cartoons for its name, since animation provides a total control that is closer to music than to live-action films."[3]

Paul's observation, meant for early sound cartoons, is illustrated even more strikingly by Disney's silents where the filmmaker had no control over music.[4] Almost all the surviving silent Disneys make the representations of music a vital part of the humor and charm of the film.

Many of Disney's cartoons, in fact, amount to silent musicals, extended comic concerts and song-and-dance routines prompted by the flimsiest of introductions. Frequently Disney even employs musical forms to structure his silent narratives. Films like *Alice the Whaler* and *Alice in the Big League* are organized like a round dance, with Alice providing the central recurring refrain, alternating with clusters of animated figures who act out assorted comic choruses. The farm in *Alice on the Farm* features what seems to be a perpetual Charleston contest. One chicken dances before a small audience, takes time out to lay a quick egg, then comes back to dance. Even before the advent of synchronized sound, Disney is organizing materials as much around music as around drama.

Music frequently plays a visual as well as audio role in the classic pursuit. Disney routinely plays off the physical shapes of notes as they appear on the printed page. In *Alice Chops the Suey*, for instance, the rodent pursuing Alice and Julius calls up reinforcements by whistling half-notes: the half-notes metamorphose into mice on roller skates. In *Alice the Fire Fighter* a rag piano player uses an octave of eighths as stepping stones up to a hotel window.

But the larger point, especially in light of the ongoing efforts to find traces of Eisenhower Disney in his early work, is that these music centerpieces are almost always the exuberant expressions of misbehavior — authority overruled. Comic anarchy reaches its fullest expression in *Alice Rattled by Rats*, a musical reworking of the old saw about what mice will do when the cat's away. In this case homeowner Alice goes out of town while house-sitter Julius is neutralized by a vat of homebrewed bootleg liquor. The mice take over, turning Alice's house into a lunatic dance hall.

Hyperkineticism prevails: everything moves. The plot, such as it is, is simply an excuse for a vaudeville concert with the threatened disruption by Julius defused when the mice get him to blow himself up. Nowhere is Disney more exuberant or inventive in showing underlings gloriously taking over the master's domain. Mice roll out the record platters, hop over the keys of the pianola, dance with the pictures on the wall, turn the bathroom shower into a musical sliding pond, and even get the intoxicated Julius to bounce off the walls to a musical beat. The film is of a piece with all those other Disney silents in which he shows kids cutting school, shoplifting and playing hookey, hoboes free from having to work, prisoners escaping prison, or Alice simply running away to have adventures. The idea of social liberation is also structured into the Disney last-minute rescue. Although there are plenty of Alices and Oswalds in which the hero rescues a damsel in distress, far more characteristic are the silent Disneys where heroes liberate captive hoards of the jailed or simply the cooped-up.

The alternative to the midwestern kingdom in silent Disney is the midwestern business dominated by the ingenious entrepreneur. As appealing as the orderly homespun kingdom was to Disney, even more congenial was the notion of a small business of some sort set on a farm or in a village. Here the drama depends upon a tension between the hard driving operator and a chorus of employees; almost invariably it involves the construction of an ingenious Rube Goldberg-type contraption or scheme related to assembly-line production. Significantly, the three or four silents in which Disney was able to smuggle fully developed narrative lines into his films — as opposed to the simple succession of gags and musical routines — all work within this formula. *Alice's Egg Plant*, for instance, pits Julius, the manager of Alice's egg farm, against his worker chickens who, led by a Bolshevik "red hen," go on strike. Julius foils the work stoppage at one assembly line —

where rows of chickens drop eggs into a conveyor belt — by creating another. He mounts a prize fight, charging his customers one egg apiece. Dutifully the hens line up and, one after another, lay their eggs at the admission gate. The mystery in *Alice Mysterious Mystery* is what has happened to the neighborhood's disappearing puppies. The answer is they have been kidnapped by a murderous but highly efficient gang who have rigged up a dog catcher truck to look like an ice cream van, ensnared their victims inside, and then poured them down a conveyor belt to an underground dungeon where they are sorted out and processed into hot dogs. Detectives Alice and Julius devise a counter stratagem involving a trap door on the sidewalk to outwit the gang and free the pups.

In the Alice comedies, the comic contraption more often than not is connected to the assembly or chorus line of look-alike animals (usually easy-to-draw mice, puppies, and fish) that Alice and Julius are expected to overpower or take in hand. In *Alice the Piper*, for instance, Alice uses a Rube Goldberg-type gigantic vacuum cleaner to sweep up the mice (and everything else in sight) before it goes berserk; in *Alice's Little Parade* she oversees a factory-like army recruitment center where a gaggle of civilian puppies walk in and columns of soldiers march out. Conversely, in *Alice and the Dog Catcher* we see a prison building where puppies enter one end and links of hot dogs emerge from the other.

But the combination of contraption and assembly line was in some ways a dead-end for Disney. In his hands, the assembly line gag seems rather perfunctory and derivative, an easy gag that all-too-obviously coasts along on labor-saving cycles, clones, and cross-overs. But the contraption gag became the mother's milk of Disney's comedy.

If early Disney silents are about anything, they are about capture and escape, and for Disney an essential part of the fun of capture/escape was creating the machinery of an elaborate ruse or punishment with which to dupe, catch, or torment one's adversary. So in the live-action prolog to *Alice's Fishy Story*, it is not enough for Alice simply to sneak out of piano practice to go fishing with her pals; she rigs up her pet German shepherd to play the piano in her place so her mother thinks she is still practicing. And where in last-minute rescue films like *Alice and the Three Bears*, *The Banker's Daughter*, and *Alice Foils the Pirates* other filmmakers might simply have locked the victim inside a cabin or tied her to a post in order to concentrate on the comic rescue efforts, Disney almost invariably inserts ingenious ghastly contrivances into the room, whether a murderous buzz-saw, a burning bootlegger's stove, or a bomb strapped to a safe dangling over the heroine's head.

The production line and Julius, the slave-driving boss in *Alice's Egg Plant*.

These last-mentioned contraptions, of course, are part of Disney's parody of stage melodrama, but the more important — and more immediate — influence is Buster Keaton. Comparing Disney's Oswald with Otto Messmer's Felix, animation historian Donald Crafton wrote in *Before Mickey*, "If Felix's balletic movements and victimization by his environment are seen as derived from Chaplin's screen character, then Oswald may be viewed as closer to Keaton and his ability to transform the absurd mechanical environment of the modern world into something useful and humane."

We may expand on Crafton's observation. Throughout Disney's silent career, his fascination with Keaton and Keaton's surreal world of machines is everywhere apparent. Not only did Disney adapt *Steamboat Bill, Jr.* for the title of his first sound Mickey Mouse, but Keaton's ingenuity in coping with a mechanized world became the dominant model for Julius and Oswald's transformations of trailer homes, cars, boats, railroads, and trolleys. Occasionally Disney was directly inspired by Keaton (the post-script in *Alice Plays Cupid* where we see former bachelor Julius now saddled with a wife and an endless procession of kids plays off the postscript in *Sherlock, Jr.*). More important are the temperamental affinities. Like Keaton, Disney's cartoon characters are inveterate tinkerers, imaginative inventors of improbable devices. But the cartoon medium permitted Disney to go even further. In late 1926 he and Ubbe Iwerks invented a cartoon character that was out of Keaton's reach, yet wholly within Keaton's domain: the mechanical animal.

The friendly robot-animal became a cornerstone in the development of Disney's craft, a wonderfully imaginative synthesis of important motifs derived from Disney's

Oswald's constant sidekick was a mechanical
animal, usually a cow, a horse, or giraffe. Here
a cow who is supposed to be in a cattle car licks
hobo Oswald's face in *Hungry Hoboes*, 1928.
(Courtesy Walt Disney Company)
Top: Frame enlargements from *The Mechanical
Cow*, 1927. (Courtesy Carlo Montanaro)

earlier work: he's an ingenious contraption, a loveable pet, a comic sidekick, and a devoted servant all rolled into one. In appearance, he owes a lot to Spark Plug, the wistful, knock-kneed race horse created in 1922 by Billy DeBeck for his "Barney Google" comic strip. The huge rolling eyes, the sausage head, breadloaf shoes, and sawhorse body were all adapted from DeBeck's creation. As a member of Disney's stock company he is arguably Disney's most original and imaginative cartoon character before Mickey Mouse; certainly he inspired many of Disney's most carefully worked out comic routines. Almost always he is a cow — an automated cow. This may reveal yet another debt to Keaton who in 1925 had used a Guernsey named Brown Eyes as a sidekick in *Go West*.

Buster Keaton and Brown Eyes in *Go West* (MGM, 1925), a source for Disney's mechanical cow. Above, another source: Billy DeBeck's Spark Plug in the popular comic strip Barney Google. Cover of sheet music from Russell Merritt Collection. Below, the forerunner of the mechanical cow: in *Alice on the Farm*, he pursues a flower in a tree.

At this point it becomes difficult to disentangle Disney from Ubbe Iwerks. To judge from internal evidence, the creation of the mechanical helper owes as much to Iwerks as it does to Disney. In the few instances where we can credit individual shots, Iwerks is invariably linked to the animation of mechanical animals, and it is probably significant that the gags introduced in the Alices and Oswalds frequently reappear in the films Iwerks animated when he left Disney in January 1930 and created Flip the Frog for Pat Powers. It is also significant that Disney's own experimentation with the mechanical animal came to a halt after Iwerks' departure. Certainly the robot-animal crystalized Iwerks' well-known enthusiasm for mechanical engineering, eccentric character movement, and bravura straight-ahead animation pyrotechnics. But this figure is no less central to Disney's development, a character that incorporated Disney's genius for personality animation, comic invention, and character design. He is an early example of Disney's ability to graft selected gestures, features, and behavioral traits of kittens and puppies onto large barnyard animals for sentimental and comical effect.

The wonderful cow in *Alice on the Farm* (January 1926) gives an idea of things to come. She is a mechanical cow *in vitro*, still anthropomorphic, but ever ready to transform herself into a piece of equipment. As a piece of animation alone, *Alice on the Farm* is a Disney benchmark. Her eccentric dance and her interaction with the field flowers set new standards for Disney's character animation. We meet the cow under a tree, smiling and snapping up flowers with her lizard-like tongue as her tail excitedly

knots and unknots. When the last flower starts to run, the cow, intrigued, crouches like a dog, wags her tail, and gives the flower a Pluto-like quizzical glance. Now cow and flower play cat and mouse: the cow stalks and pounces, the flower reacts. Finally, flower jumps onto a low branch of the tree; the cow jumps up too, pounces on the flower, and eats it. Satisfied, she relaxes in the tree, rests her cheek on a front hoof *Venus Victrix*-like, and, smiling, chews her cud.

But Iwerks has just started. Moments later, the cow transforms herself into a wireless radio, raising her tail and one of her horns that in turn sprout radio wire to create an antenna. That completed, the cow pulls off her other horn and uses it like an earphone.

Message received, the cow jumps out of a tree (one of Disney's earliest cuts on action, the cow jumping into frame as she lands), and goes into a demented dance: a buck-and-wing complicated by a few somersaults, a high-stepping prance, and a sideway shuffle.

For a moment it looks as though the dance will continue when the cow joins up with Julius: they bow to each other as though ready to start a minuet. Instead, the cow turns herself into a milk pump, tucking her hind leg behind her ear to give Julius access to her udder, Julius using her tail as a crank to pump out the milk.

Alice's Brown Derby.
(Courtesy Nederlands Filmmuseum)

Iwerks and Disney experimented fitfully with the personality of secondary characters like their cow in the Alices that followed, but the mechanical animal comes into its own only with the invention of Oswald eighteen months later. Up to that point, Disney's concern with mechanical animals is sheerly technical. The "fake" hobby horse that competes with "real" horses in the assorted Alice race films (notably in *Alice Wins the Derby*, July 1925, and *Alice's Brown Derby*, December 1926) is generally used as simple counterpoint, its staccato 4-drawing cycle meant to highlight the flow of the "real" horses' 8- and 9-drawing run, for which Iwerks took great pains to capture the undulating tail and even rhythms of the galloping legs.

In the Oswald cartoons, however, the mechanical animal develops into a full-blown animated character, frequently cast as Oswald's side-kick and a permanent part of the Oswald repertory company. His official debut is in *The Mechanical Cow*, the fourth Oswald release, which appeared in early October 1927. The animation itself shows little progress from *Alice on the Farm*. Iwerks and his co-workers have not yet discovered the principles of overlapping motion, follow-through, or secondary actions, so that there is little to distinguish the movements of the mechanical cow from the stiff, unnatural movements of Oswald and the other characters. Here as elsewhere in the surviving Oswalds, when one part of the body moves, all the other body parts freeze.

But as a fresh personality, the cow is a wonderfully supple character. Iwerks and Disney have blended together several distinct roles for him that dovetail seamlessly as the cartoon speeds through its acts. The cow is Oswald's ingenious invention, but first and foremost he is a winsome companion. Throughout the cartoon, the filmmakers are careful to subordinate the mechanical gags to routines that establish the cow's shy, playful personality. So, for example, at the start Oswald and the Cow sleep together in bed, their friendship instantly established with their snoring. As one inhales, the other exhales, and together their bodies move up and down under the covers like alternating pistons. When Oswald wakes up and throws off the blankets, we see that the cow is a robot, but it acts as though it were human — it sticks a finger in its ear, rumples its face, yawns and stretches, and doesn't want to get out of bed.

Once Oswald moves his contraption down into the street, we watch how the Cow works as a mechanical invention — a futuristic milk machine. What follows derives from the kind of vaudeville routine patented by Keaton and Fields. A passing Hippo wants milk for her baby and Oswald sets the Cow up as a gas-pump. Don Crafton describes the rest of the scene: "Oswald opens a trapdoor on the cow's back and erects a glass 'tank' into which he pumps milk. In a closeup, Oswald checks the baby's 'level' with a dipstick and sees it is running low. So, in another long shot, he stretches out an enormous teat and pumps milk into the baby. Mrs. Hippo departs, another satisfied customer."[5]

Now, when Oswald meets his sweetheart, the cow is set off on another track. Now he is Oswald's devoted pet, licking his owner's face with his oversize tongue, craving his master's attention. For Oswald, who wants to be alone with Sweetie, the cow's a pest and he orders the cow to leave. The puppy-like cow sadly obeys and, head drooping and his broomstick tail dragging behind him, wanders off disconsolate.

Within moments, however, Oswald's sweetheart is kidnapped, so when the cow reappears, it is in the guise of a snorting wonder horse, fearlessly dodging bullets as he carries Oswald on his back (the film synopsis notes that Oswald "rides him like Tom Mix"). The wonder cow swallows a speeding cannonball and blows up, but his parts fall miraculously back into place. As a robotic marvel, he has other advantages: he comes with detachable parts that Oswald uses to deflect bullets; an expanding neck that works like an extension ladder; and interchangeable parts so that Oswald can reverse directions by simply switching the Cow's head and tail.

Then in a final twist, the mechanical animal becomes his master's rescuer by engineering a clever trick of his own. Oswald and his sweetheart have fallen over a cliff, hanging by a branch over shark-infested waters. How to get them back to firm ground? The Cow thinks fast. He sees the villain's taxi charging at him and contorts his body into a ramp. The car speeds over the ramp and over the cliff out of control, crashes into the sea, and creates a gushing plume of water that works like an elevator to transport Oswald and Sweetie back to firm ground. Delighted to see his friends again, the Cow opens up a rumble seat on his back and pushes off with the happy couple into the sunset.

This was as clever and as appealing a secondary character as Disney had invented up to that time, and in the months that followed, he regularly returned to his mechanical animal to explore further possibilities. In design, he was both a complement and a foil to Oswald. His barrel body, pointed horns, and angular joints played against the soft rubbery Oswald. But his floppy ears, huge gunboat shoes and the Felix-like face mask suggested that, visually at least, he and Oswald were cartoon kin.

In certain ways, the mechanical animal became Disney's response to the increasingly surrealistic look of the Felix and the Out-of-the-Inkwell cartoons. Eventually, of course, Disney's gamut of romantic styles would all but eclipse the surrealism of Max Fleischer and Otto Messmer. But in the 1920s, their influence on Disney was particularly pronounced. Significantly, however, when Disney, the least surreal of animators, figured out how to absorb this alien, uncongenial style into his work, it was by incorporating it into character design and behavior, not through environmental distortion. Despite his fondness for bootleg liquor gags, for instance, he almost never tried his hand at the

The road not taken. Despite his fondness for bootleg liquor gags, Disney avoided the surrealistic nightmare imagery of rivals Dave Fleischer and Otto Messmer. From *Sure-Locked Homes* (below left) and *Felix Woos Whoopee* (below right), released in the late 1920s.

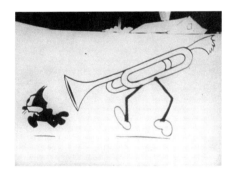

W. C. Fields, who inspired the Blind Pig gag in *Rickety Gin*. From Paramount's *"That Royle Girl"*, 1925. (Courtesy Academy of Motion Picture Arts and Sciences)

surrealistic hallucination or *delirium tremens* sequence patented by Felix. His one effort at the drunken nightmare is part of a lost 1928 Oswald called *Rickety Gin* where, judging from the script, he simply copied the brilliant surrealistic metamorphoses in *Felix Woos Whoopee* (the gin bottle, according to the script, changes into "snakes, a spider, a hideous-looking dragon, large bats with big claws, a two-headed dragon spitting fire, an ugly genie," and so forth). Instead, Disney found his strength in personality design where he could cannibalize a wide variety of influences and create highly original effects.

So, for instance, when the mechanical animal next appears in *The Ocean Hop*, Disney returns to the race track formula popularized in the "Barney Google" comic strip. Here the animal is a dummy horse styled after Spark Plug. The twist is that this horse with some minor adjustments can fly, powered by mice inside its belly who flap its mechanical wings.

In *Rickety Gin* (January, 1928), he returns as a mechanical Blind Pig, now attached to Oswald's nemesis, Putrid Pete. This may be the mechanical animal's most maniacal permutation. The film itself, as we mentioned earlier, has been lost. But the surviving script and gag synopsis give us a detailed idea of what Disney had in mind. As Pete's sidekick, the Blind Pig seems merely another member of the gang, a tough-looking sightless animal wearing dark glasses and using a cane to guide himself. When the coast is clear, however, the Pig for no apparent reason attracts the interest of a surprisingly eager group of by-standers. He is in fact a walking vending cart from which Pete dispenses bootleg liquor — a moveable saloon. But the Pig has special features. Most importantly, it dispenses atmosphere. So while Pete dispenses liquor from the Pig's tongue and snout, the Pig's torso rolls out to become a tiny footrail and a hind hoof detaches itself for a cuspidor. With each purchase, the customer is treated to a shoeshine from the tiny hands that shoot out from the rail, while Pete sprinkles a soupcon of sawdust around about for good measure.

W. C. Fields had created a near-identical routine with a baby carriage in the stage play *Poppy* which Disney probably saw as the 1925 movie *Sally of the Sawdust*. But from this point, Disney takes off on his own, creating a kind of barnyard surrealism that became an early signature. In *Rival Romeos* (February 1928) he invents the mechanical goat gag that would become world-famous later in the year when he recycled it for *Steamboat Willie*. Halfway through the film a goat eats Oswald's sheet music and banjo. Ever able to rise to the occasion, Oswald plays the goat like a hurdy-gurdy, cranking his tail while a stream of notes float out of his mouth. In *Ride 'em Plowboy!* (April 1928) Disney constructs the first of his midwestern cyclones, sending Oswald up in the sky with the cow he is milking, then having him save himself by converting the cow into an ersatz airplane.

The next logical step follows: Oswald himself becomes a part-time mechanical. At first, the machine-like limb is just another expressive body part. So when Oswald's legs turn into a pair of elevator rails in *The Fox Chase*, carrying his torso down into the depths of his trousers, then up into the clouds, the gag is entertaining but unremarkable. But starting with *Ozzie of the Mounted* (produced in January 1928), where mountie Oswald rides a mechanical horse, Oswald's transformations take strikingly grotesque and painful turns. When Pete pulls out Oswald's tongue, yards of it uncoil and the tongue takes on a life of its own. According to an early continuity draft, the tongue transforms itself into a lariat, lassoes the runaway bandit, and drags its hapless owner along as Pete continues to run. Later in the film, Oswald's hobby horse bursts a spring which is welded to Oswald's posterior, so that when Oswald catches his chin on a tree branch, the runaway horse elongates the spring, choking and then firing Oswald like a pellet in a slingshot.

The new emphasis on pain and distress associated with the mechanical body is particularly evident in the surviving scripts. Here, for example, is a description of shot #17 in *Hungry Hoboes* where Pete turns Oswald into a mechanical monkey: "Pete grabs him [Oswald], pulls his arms out long — then as he pulls Oswald's tail out, it [the motion] pulls his ears in — and by choking Oswald he makes his eyes and face bulge out like [a] monkey — Oswald protests but Pete bullies him into it — puts string around Oswald's neck, chokes him, and starts turning crank."

Here is how the humanoid steam shovel behaves in *Sky Scrappers*:

Shot 1: [We see] a big mechanical monster with large teeth — big eyes and nostrils (it's a big steam shovel — exhaust pipes for nostrils — large washers with nuts in center for eyes). As its lower jaw drops open, steam shoots out nostrils as it moves away from camera ....

It bites in dirt with sort of human actions — its rear wheels stretch up and raise body up so that it can get a good mouthful — body wiggles in human fashion as it digs in dirt ....

When dirt lands in truck, it smashes body down and flattens rear wheels — [and] raises front end of truck up off ground (not too much) — then the truck does pained human crawl off scene ....

In short, even before the early Mickey, Disney and Iwerks were cultivating their taste for the macabre and sadistic. Almost imperceptibly, they have moved from the sweet, joyful flavor of Barney Google and Spark Plug to the darker elemental anarchy of the first Mickeys, where the mechanical animal can be exploited as a helpless puppet or domineering tyrant, simple and unsentimental.

From the start, critics have viewed the Oswalds as an improvement over the Alices because of their technical polish: the faster pace, tighter construction, and their kinetic sense of space. Disney himself wrote enthusiastically about Oswald, telegraphing Mintz in February 1927, "Up to the present time I have felt we have been in a rut regarding style and general construction of our plots and gags. Now I believe I have found 'IT.' Wish you would take special notice of the future pictures and let me know just what you think."

Part of "it" was his conscious decision to move towards the stylistic conventions of live-action films. Increasingly, the cutting patterns of his cartoons imitated the editing conventions of the silent feature; so did his simulated camera movements, simulated iris masks, and point of view shots. The trend had started, in fact, with the middle Alices in which he began working with cross-cutting and match-on-action to improve the staging of his gags. As early as April 1924, for instance, he cross-cut in *Alice's Fishy Story* between Julius swimming underwater pursued by a shark and Alice talking with an Eskimo ice fisherman. The cross-cutting sharpens the punchline: Julius erupting through the hole onto the ice to disrupt Alice and the fisherman. A few months later, in *Alice Cans the Cannibals*, Disney combined diagonally-angled shots and multiple camera set-ups to make more dynamic his opening gag sequence. Alice and Julius are marooned atop their sinking car when Julius lassoes a dolphin and dangles a flirtatious worm in his face so the car can be towed across the frame. To create spatial variety and to dramatize the visual contrast between the bulky car and the leaping fish, Disney alternates between two master shots, each taken from behind the car and angling the car off 45° to the rear so that the fish can be seen frolicking in the distance off to the side of the frame. Cutting in and out to *faux*-iris close ups and two-shots of Julius, the dolphin, and the worm, Disney uses no fewer than seven shots before the dolphin tugs the car off-screen. Temporally more nuanced, *Alice the Jail Bird*, completed in late August 1925, constructs a gag dependent on a cut-away used to imply a passage of time. A prison guard, furious at Alice, pounds his fist on a stump. Julius, making practical use of the wasted fist motion, puts boulders on the stump so that the guard's fist will crush them. Cut away to a turtle, in another part of the jail yard, shooting pool with the rocks he's supposed to be cracking. Return to the guard in medium shot, his fist now swathed in a giant bandage, still yelling at Alice.

Combination shot gags multiply in the 1925 Alices, and by the end of the year glance-object editing patterns are a regular part of the Disney repertoire. More dramatic, however, is the simulation of live-action *mise-en-scène* effects, particularly the use of shadows and the play with false perspective in background drawings. Like energy and sweat lines, inconspicuous body shadows were used sporadically in the earliest Alices, and by 1926 were used whenever time and budget permitted. In the remarkable *Alice Picks the Champ*, animated in spring 1925, shadows even take on a story-telling

Increasingly, Disney turned to live-action movies for inspiration, especially the work of Keaton, Fairbanks, Lloyd, and Tom Mix. In *Alice Picks the Champ*, Disney plays off Fairbanks' use of shadows in action scenes. Below: *The Mechanical Cow*. (Courtesy Carlo Montanaro)

function. Julius has been put in a boxing ring with "Tough Pete," who has pulverized all previous contenders. Julius' fight, the climax of the film, is dramatized entirely through the boxer's elongated shadows on the wall. We see one of the fighters knocked out, but because of the distortion the shadows provide, we can't tell which fighter has been left standing. Outside the door, waiting for the winner to emerge, Alice is left in suspense and so are we.

One suspects that here Disney was recalling the startling use of shadows in the climactic dueling scene of Fairbanks' *Robin Hood*. More specific and even more remarkable is his use of what he found in Victor Seastrom's vehicle for Lon Chaney, *He Who Gets Slapped*. Midway through *Alice's Circus Daze*, Disney shows an extreme close-up of a laughing clown, directly patterned on the opening close-up of Chaney, but he adds a blurry background in order to simulate the narrow focal range of the telephoto lens!

In short, by the time he started his Oswald series, Disney had already gone a long way in incorporating and adapting live-action Hollywood conventions. But the Oswald series marks an unprecedented intensification of effort. The number of shots per film multiplies as does the variety of simulated camera set-ups; temporal transitions are marked by graphic and rhythmic matches; simulated camera movements grow more complex as do the movements of the characters themselves. Two late Alices, *Alice's Brown Derby* and *Alice the Fire Fighter*, use twenty-four and thirty-two shots respectively; within six months, Disney is breaking down two early Oswalds, *The Mechanical Cow* and *Great Guns*, into forty-four and forty-eight shots. He uses straightforward lateral movements less and less, favoring instead diagonal directions and, even more, weaving patterns of motion that guide characters towards and away from the camera as they run across the screen. Disney becomes particularly enamoured with the into-the-camera shot where a character moves into an extreme close-up and, still moving, blacks out the frame. Point-of-view shots begin to proliferate too, frequently providing the occasion for distinctive masks and oblique angles.

Disney's staging of comic scenes was also growing closer to his live-action screen models. Not just Keaton, but Fairbanks, Harold Lloyd, Laurel and Hardy, and Chaplin were gradually eclipsing Krazy Kat, Felix, and Koko as Disney's dominant models.

Under their influence, he was moving away from the rapid-fire succession of gags towards carefully worked-out situational humor, building on a gag, working on details, making the gag pay off before moving to another scene. Increasingly, he played with the feelings of characters involved in the gags. Compare, for instance, a fight-and-chase scene in *Alice Picks the Champ*, one of the great 1926 Alices, with a similar scene from the 1927 Oswald, *Great Guns*.

Julius' first encounter with Tough Pete in *Alice Picks the Champ* is staged in vintage twenties cartoon-comic strip fashion. Julius looks on, dumb-struck (i.e. stock still, with a single open-mouthed expression) while his formidable adversary shadow boxes and growls, demonstrating his overwhelming ferocity. When the bear turns and points his come-hither finger at Julius, the cat registers cartoon terror: painted sweat droplets shower out of his head, his knees knock, and his torso undulates. The single change of expression is to a sickly sweet smile, then a return to the look of open-mouth wonder. The bear suddenly expands to Brobdingnagian proportions, growls, and Julius tears off — running so quickly that he forgets his head. A funny fast-paced sequence, it is built entirely on cartoon slapstick and visual tricks.

The comparable scene in *Great Guns*, on the other hand, is constructed almost entirely around personality clashes. At a moment when Oswald, like Julius, realizes he is about to be pulverized by a Goliath, Disney analyzes and extends the psychological implications of the moment. In this instance, Oswald has been caught red-handed gleefully trying to strangle an enemy mouse. Preoccupied with wringing the mouse's neck, he is unaware that an enormous upright rodent has crept up behind him. Oswald gets the message when he responds to the rodent's tapping foot: he pauses, turns his head, looks at the rat's foot, then, still holding firm to the mouse, slowly scans this stranger's body. Oswald's look of ferocity gives way to a sheepish grin. What's this he has in his hands? Why it's his friend, of course. He pets the mouse on the head, eyes rolling back and forth from one rodent to the other. The rat isn't buying, continuing to work his foot, hands on hips. Oswald gently lets the mouse go, looks offended and surprised when the mouse points an accusing finger at him, then turns coy. Thrusting his hands in his pockets, he rocks back and forth, slowly starts shuffling off to the far side of the screen, sweetly waving good-bye. The rodent lunges; Oswald shoots off. There's nothing here, of course, that Laurel and Hardy hadn't done before with Edgar Kennedy, but what is of interest is Disney's shift of emphasis from the chase to the initial encounter, emphasizing the strong changes of attitude and expression in Oswald, from the first gasp of recognition to his struggle to gain composure. Disney would polish the scene with Mickey Mouse first in *Barnyard Battle*, then in *The Pointer*, but this new direction starts in the silents.

The one thing that did not seem to evolve much was the animation itself. It's no good contending, as several historians have, that Disney abandoned labor-saving cycles, cross-overs, and repeat actions for a more open-ended straight-ahead style. Quite the contrary, cycles play as much a role in the Oswalds as they do in the Alices. And despite the strides made in character design, staging, and diagonal movement, Oswald and his companions appear as stiff and unnatural as Julius and his cronies, their movements still segmented, their creators still wedded to the rubber hose limbs. As yet neither Disney nor his colleagues have developed any interest in anatomy or musculature, nor any detailed curiosity about the way creatures or things actually move. When Oswald wants to reach something, his arms merely grow. When he's happy, he jumps for joy, but without effort, thrust or weight. As Frank Thomas and Ollie Johnston wrote in *Disney Animation: The Illusion of Life*, still the best book on Disney animation, the silent Disney animators conceived of their job in terms of creating direct, sprightly movements that put their gags over. Curiously, for all the discussion of Disney's attention to personality animation, the most adventurous experiments in movement were reserved for hand props, buildings, and other ordinarily inanimate objects. Early in the Alice series, he develops a feel for animatable objects, making the simplest of shapes expressive by squashing and stretching them. The villain bear's top hat in *Alice Stage Struck*, for instance, develops a personality of its own as it twists and turns, jumps and hides,

Technically, Disney's silent animation never got much beyond the rubber hose conventions. From *Alice the Whaler*. Opposite: A late vestige of the mechanical cow in *Steamboat Willie*. (Copyright Walt Disney Company)

ducking the snowballs Alice and Julius toss at it. The most flexible, pliable shape in *Alice Plays Cupid* is the steepled church where Julius marries his sweetheart. The church swells and contracts, the steeple bounces up and down, while the bell clangs, the embodiment of the happy day. Recent historians have drawn attention to the libidinous aspects of these structural interplays, tumescent cannons that fall into flaccid exhaustion after they fire, tower steeples that wave to and fro, bayonets that curlicue, and so forth. But we may also notice that this play with volume, mass, and gravity is also forerunner to — in fact, the basis of — Disney's breakthrough as a character animator, the earliest application of the famous squash and stretch principles that in the 1930s started breathing life into his animal figures and human caricatures.

Those accustomed to thinking of Mickey Mouse and *Steamboat Willie* as Disney's starting point tend to view Disney's progress as a satiric American success story: the brilliant, scrappy iconoclast who flourished and then became bland, the comic whirlwind force that ended as an avuncular TV host. But those who chart Disney's career from Kansas City six years earlier may see a rather different kind of story. This Disney does not begin as an unbridled free spirit, nor does he start creating libidinous, rambunctious, characters. Rather Disney, the gregarious teen-age military veteran, is a polite, deferential mid-westerner who makes sing-alongs and sweet-tempered comedies about a little girl and her animal friends. The effervescent spirit of elemental anarchy that permeates the first Mickeys comes only later, acquired as Disney gains more experience in the ferociously

Scene # 29.

Medium shot of little girl turning goats tail like crank....and music of ' Turkey in the Straw ' comes out his mouth like hand organ....

As she cranks che does crazy clog dance........

Scene # 30.

C.U. of Mickey drumming on bucket Old cows head sticking in left side of scene....she is chewing in time to music.....she reaches over and licks Mickeys face with her long tongue....then smiles (shows teeth) Mickey sees teeth....opens her mouth wide and hammers on her teeth like playing Xylophone....plays in time to music....runs up and down scale, etc.
      Just as he is about to finish two large feet(the Captains) walk into right side of scene and stop....Mickey finishes piece with 'Ta-da-de-da-da-... on cows horns....pulls out her tongue and strums 'Dum - Dum...' on it...and turns around to girl with smile....He sees feet...looks upslowly...when he sees its Captain he acts surprised...

Painless mutilation of the body. Julius loses his skin in *Alice Chops the Suey*; Julius detaches his face in *Alice Gets Stung*.

competitive animation business. In this regard, Oswald is a genuine precursor to Mickey, not so much in appearance as in behavior and in internal dynamics. Noted children's writer Maurice Sendak once said about the early Mickey Mouse, "Look at those early cartoons. They're all about body parts: kicking the ass, pulling the ears, tweaking noses, twisting necks. It's the kind of passionate investigation of the body which is part of the nature of the child."

The same can be said of Disney's Oswald. Central to his construction and animation is the heightened sense of touch and resilient plasticity. As Sendak says of early Mickey, "he gives you license to touch. There is something eminently gropable about him. He's like a baby. Everybody loves to hold a baby, to touch it, to kiss it, to lick it."[6]

The crucial key to this "license to touch" is Oswald's new-found capacity to register a response to what is happening to his body. Like Mickey, when Oswald's body is twisted, stretched, or tweaked, Oswald hurts. His mouth opens wide, his eyes roll or squint, his face squeezes. When he is tickled, he giggles. He is, like his predecessors, made up of crazy parts that will bend and detach, but the crucial distinction is that he responds to physical stimuli in humanly recognizable ways.

This is quite different from what happens with Alice's Julius. Julius, of course, also has expressive body parts. He is forever losing his head, tearing off his face, detaching his tail walking out of his skin, and splitting himself in half. But there are no somatic consequences. Mostly these are demonstrations of the cat's (and the animator's) inventiveness; Julius' classic response is to turn towards the camera and grin. The most discomfort Julius ever feels is embarrassment when he is denuded of his black skin. He seldom if ever registers pain. When he crashes on the pavement or runs into a brick wall, the symbols are so detached from him — stars or birds circling around his head — and the after-effect so fleeting that he requires no comforting or stroking.

But the darkening of Disney's world corresponds with his discovery of looser character animation. As he expands the ways the body can be stretched, squeezed, and twisted, he also makes characters aware of their bodies, the way their bodies can give them pleasure and pain. When Oswald twists off his left hind leg to kiss it in *Hungry Hoboes* (he's about to enter a fight and needs the luck of the rabbit foot), his face first screws up in anguish, and then, as he contemplates the foot, he holds it up against his cheek and gently strokes it. That brief but remarkable gesture, with its hint of eroticism, violence, and infantile self-discovery, points to the shape of things to come. By the end of the year, Disney left the silents forever and learned how to make his barnyard animals chortle, squeak, giggle, bellow, sing, and cry.

This is how the silent period ended for Disney. We now turn to how it began. In 1921, Disney was still an apprentice in a commercial art studio in Kansas City, moonlighting by animating newsreel fillers for a local movie theater. In the chapters that follow, we will pursue his career from those earliest efforts — the creation of the first Laugh-O-grams for Frank Newman's theaters — through his first silent Mickey Mouse cartoons. In the course of that history, we will try to chart not only how he developed his distinctive cartoon products, but also how he built his business and his public image.

Notes

1. Quoted in Frank Thomas and Ollie Johnston, *Disney Animation: The Illusion of Life*, New York: Abbeville, 1981, 35.

2. Winkler to Disney 1/9/24; Winkler to Disney 1/31/24; Disney to Winkler 9/29/24; Disney to Mintz 12/2/24; George Winkler to Disney 8/11/25; George Winkler to Disney 9/4/25; Mintz to Disney 5/20/26. Disney business correspondence survives at the Walt Disney Archives.

3. William Paul, "Art, Music, Nature, and Walt Disney," *Movie* 24 (Summer 1970), 44.

4. As far as we can tell, no music was ever sent out with either the Disney Alices or Disney Oswalds. No reference to music survives in either the correspondence or business records. The single cue sheet to survive — for *Alice's Brown Derby* — was likely meant for the Raytone 1931 reissue.

5. Donald Crafton, *Before Mickey*, MIT Press, 1982, 295.

6. From an interview with Russell Merritt, incorporated into Karen and Russell Merritt, "Mythic Mouse," *Griffithiana* 34 (December 1988), 58-71.

Newman Laugh-O-grams

The artist seats himself at his drawing board, lights his pipe, picks up a pen and goes to work. His manner is confident. Nattily dressed and surrounded by the trappings of the successful young executive, he looks as if he knows he will revolutionize an industry and an art form within two decades. This is Walt Disney, age nineteen, and — with a near-prophetic sense of history — he is making a rare on-screen appearance at the beginning of his first theatrical motion picture.

Like his contemporaries, Disney discarded the image of the animator-as-magician that had characterized the pre-war generation of sketch artists. Rather, in his 1921 debut he presents himself as the bright young entrepreneur, the bemused artist at his desk, the hard-working editorial cartoonist. The first drawing, it might be noted, is also of himself — a caricature of the artist as a young man at the margin of the main title card. The caricature reinforces the live-action image: a figure of an earnest young man with unkempt hair working intently, doing everything himself, the pages flying off his desk. Disney was carefully cultivating this image at the time; the same caricature was used on his business card, and would reappear in the trade advertisements for his first animation studio in 1922.

Three views of the artist as a fledgling animator: Walt Disney drawn by Walt Disney on the corner of an envelope (top) and on the title card of the *Newman Laugh-O-gram* sample reel (above); Walt Disney directed by Walt Disney in the *Newman Laugh-O-gram* sample reel (right).
Following pages: Young illustrator Disney posing at his drawing board. He worked on short films, stop-motion animation, and slides for local theaters while at Kansas City Film Ad.
Ubbe Iwerks, Walt Disney, and Fred Harman, Kansas City, c. 1921.
(Courtesy Walt Disney Company)

The Kansas City Film Advertising Company in 1920, seed bed for Disney's animation company. Disney is seated in the back row, smoking a pipe, next to Fred Harman. In the row in front of him, second from left, Ubbe Iwerks. (Courtesy Walt Disney Company)

Fred Harman, Walt Disney, and Red Lyon at Kansas City Film Ad. (Courtesy Walt Disney Company)

The cartoon he is making — the cartoon we are watching him make — was a sample reel for a local Kansas City theater chain controlled by Frank L. Newman, the city's leading exhibitor. Disney's idea was to win a place in the program of newsreels, comedy shorts, and vaudeville acts that Newman booked into his theaters each week. The Newman Laugh-O-gram was meant to mix advertising with topical humor of local interest. The basic format of the pictures, that of a lightning-fast sketch artist commenting on local news stories, combined animation with rapidly drawn sketches that commented on current foibles and events. The sample reel, for example, editorialized on Kansas City's current crime problem, the disrepair of the streets, latest fashions, and (in the single animated sequence) a current police department shake-up. This last sequence is of immeasurable historical value today because it is fully animated by Walt Disney himself. In all his other surviving films from the Kansas City period, the time-consuming labor of animation is shared by other hands; and Disney would personally withdraw from animation altogether soon after his arrival in Hollywood. But this short scene is his work alone.

In style there is nothing revolutionary about these pictures. The idea of a hand sketching a figure and bringing it to life was already an animation tradition by 1921, going back to the turn-of-the-century lightning sketch artists and widely imitated since Bobby Bumps was introduced by animator Earl Hurd's hand in the Teens. Of course, it was also a device the Fleischer brothers would soon explore in their Out of the Inkwell series. But Disney sought a fresh approach by using his sketches to comment on local affairs, making them an animated counterpart to the locally produced newsreels that were cropping up in communities across the country. The Laugh-O-gram sample reel, for instance, refers to the winter 1920-21 Kansas City police corruption scandal, reported in the *Kansas City Star*, February 6, 1921.

Animated shorts such as Disney's did not displace live-action comics from the screen (as Mickey Mouse would later do), but rather coexisted with them. The same week Newman booked Disney's sample reel into the Newman Theatre on 20 March 1921, he was booking a Christie comedy at his New Royal Theatre, competing with Keaton's *The Goat* at the Linwood, an Al St. John Sunshine Comedy at the Apollo, and a Douglas Fairbanks comedy feature, *The Nut*, at the Liberty. The Laugh-O-grams appeared only occasionally in the following months — Disney was producing them single-handedly — and then in the form of isolated segments which were sandwiched in among the other newsreels. In addition, Newman filled in his programs with Toonerville Trolley and Larry Semon comedies, and short concerts by musical director Leo M. Forbstein (later head of the Warner Bros. music department).

Among other things, the Newman reel eventually brought Disney his first contact with a man who was himself destined to leave a mark on animation: Rudolph Ising. Ising later recalled that he answered a newspaper ad which promised to teach aspiring cartoonists the craft of animation. He found himself assisting Disney with the Newman shorts; he recalled that Disney was then calling his organization "Kay-Cee Studios."

It has been noted elsewhere that, for the sketch-artist films, the hand which seemed to be doing the sketching was actually a *photograph* of a hand, since Disney's hand would not fit between the camera lens and the paper. Ising confirmed that the hand was a photo, but pointed out that it was used for reasons, not of space, but of focus. "Here's your platen," he explained, "and there's the camera, about there, focused on this thing. So a hand would be completely out of focus at that range." By the time Ising started working on the films, a basic technique had been established. Disney, working at night (for he was still employed at Kansas City Film Ad during the day), would make the full drawing in light blue pencil, which would not photograph on orthochromatic film. Then Ising would put the drawing beneath the camera and move the hand photo along the outlines of the drawing, inking them in as he went, and exposing frames at successive stages. He remembered that Disney was shooting his films on positive stock for increased contrast, a practice he would continue throughout most of the silent period.

After this first Newman Laugh-O-gram, what was the content of the others? If available recollections are any guide, they consisted largely of more of the same. Ising

Title card for the Laugh-O-gram series. (Courtesy Walt Disney Company)

remembered that he and Disney continued to take humorous note of local happenings. "Like when the police department decided to have horse police, for instance, we called it horsing around town." Subsequent pictures also included advertising. In later years Disney proudly recalled one ad, for auto top replacements, to both his daughter Diane and his brother-in-law Bill Cottrell. In this ad two friends meet beside a car. The first man says: "Hi, old top, new car?" Second man: "No, new top, old car."

Aside from the sample reel, none of the Newman Laugh-O-grams are known to survive.

Laugh-O-gram Films

It was not in Walt Disney's nature to be satisfied for long with Newman Laugh-O-grams. Despite their success, he was eager to try something more substantial: a narrative cartoon. Such a film would, of course, be a daunting undertaking for a lone animator. Accordingly, Disney began to place ads in local newspapers, offering to teach budding cartoonists the art of animation — an art to which Disney himself was little more than a stranger. (It was one of these ads which first attracted Rudy Ising.) Working in the evenings, and proceeding slowly — for he was still employed at Kansas City Film Ad during the day, and was still turning out Newman Laugh-O-grams on a regular basis — Disney and his student/assistant animators began work on a modernized cartoon version of *Little Red Riding Hood*.

How could Disney, with only the slightest beginning knowledge of animation, undertake to teach it to others? He relied heavily on a book, which he had picked up at Kansas City Film Ad, called *Animated Cartoons: How They Are Made, Their Origin and Development*, written by E. G. Lutz in 1920. This book was an indispensable guide not only for Film Ad animators, but for the animation industry at large. Its influence on Disney during these years cannot be overestimated. Lutz offered basic information on anatomy and movement and on technical aspects of motion pictures, but the bulk of his book consisted of labor-saving devices and shortcuts. "Of all the talents required by any one going into this branch of art," he wrote, "none is so important as that of the skill to plan the work so that the lowest possible number of drawings need be made for any particular scenario." Here Disney learned how to perform the tricks of the trade — cycles, cutout animation, the "slash" system, how to hold and repeat drawings.

The discovery of this book so early in his professional life was of particular importance to Disney's career. American animators of the silent era can be loosely divided into two camps. In one, directly descended from the animators of the Praxinoscope and other pre-cinematic toys, is Winsor McCay, the creator of Little Nemo and Gertie the Dinosaur. McCay's creative genius and passion for hard work led him to labor painstakingly over his films with little or no assistance, scorning any labor-saving methods. His films were richly detailed and beautiful — and, not uncommonly, took months on end to produce. The other camp can be represented by J. R. Bray, of Col. Heeza Liar fame, who sought to produce animated films quickly and cheaply by applying assembly-line methods. Bray's films were hardly the works of art that McCay's were, but he was able to crank them out with such speed and consistency as to release them to theaters on a regular basis. He transformed animation into a viable business and, not surprisingly, became the model for most American animation producers. Lutz's book never mentions Bray by name, but it codifies his methods as *the* way to produce animated cartoons.

Disney unhesitatingly accepted the Bray-Lutz principles, eagerly embracing the use of time-saving tricks. His early films, for example, make liberal use of cycles, cleverly devised to *suggest* elaborate action. But Disney added a twist: he strove from the first for an ever-higher standard of quality on the screen — better drawings, more and better gags, abundant detail. By the mid-thirties he had refined and synthesized the concepts of Bray and McCay. The Disney studio was by then a "factory" like the others, one which could release films on a regular schedule. But this "factory" was built to support a great number of individual artists, and designed to promote the development and growth of each one. Disney's approach was vindicated, if need be, by its results; Winsor McCay, as brilliant as he was, could never have produced *Fantasia* by his own methods.

After six months *Little Red Riding Hood* was finally finished, and Disney and his fellow artists were sufficiently encouraged to tackle another production, *The Four Musicians of Bremen*. Disney was by now fully committed to animation, and in the spring of 1922 he made two decisive moves. He quit his Film Ad job; and, his expanding staff having outgrown the family garage, he rented an office. His company's new quarters were on the second floor of the McConahy Building, a new office building at 1127 East 31st Street. They consisted of two partitioned offices at the head of the stairs. Disney was now ready to go into business in a serious way.

There was, of course, a major drawback to being self-employed: Disney had no income. As his rent and grocery bills continued to mount, this became a serious matter. "I knew Walt was having a hard time," Rudy Ising recalled. "A guy came up one day and said, 'Is Mr. Dinsey' — D-I-N-S-E-Y, that was the way he pronounced it — 'here?' And Walt said, 'No, I don't think so.' And he said, 'Well, I'll be back,' and went on down the stairs again. That's when Walt told me it was a process server. And sure enough it was, because the guy came back for, oh, a couple of weeks. And Walt and I were the only ones there, so he'd say, 'Is Walt Dinsey here?' And if Walt was there he'd say, 'No, he hasn't shown up today,' or if it was me I'd do the same thing." How long this evasion might have lasted is open to speculation, but it was undone by a visit from Disney's long-time friend Walt Pfeiffer. "I guess Walt Pfeiffer and Walt Disney were just talking away, looking at some drawings or visiting or something. And the guy came up, and before he had a chance to say anything, Walt Pfeiffer says, 'Now listen, Walt,' and so on and so on." Ising chuckled at the memory. "The guy looked at him, and Walt said, 'Yeah — I'm Walt Dinsey. But my name is Disney, not Dinsey!'"

This incident served to impress Ising with the enormity of Disney's debts. "I had been working for three or four years and I had saved up about a thousand dollars — I don't know how I did it. And it ended up, I loaned him five hundred dollars to bail him out on a couple of these things." Shortly afterward, Disney hit on a better way to put his business on a solid financial footing: he decided to incorporate. "And Walt decided," said Ising, "that rather than pay me back, he'd give me stock in the corporation. And he talked me into it. He was quite a salesman." The new company was capitalized at $15,000. "But by the time the broker took his cut," Ising added, "I think they only got about, out of fifteen, they got about six to eight thousand dollars. So both Walt and I and a couple of the guys were still working for practically nothing for a long time."

The new company's certificate of incorporation was issued by the state of Missouri on 23 May 1922. Taking its cue from Disney's films for the Newman chain, the company was christened Laugh-O-gram Films, Inc. The new Laugh-O-grams were to be a series of fairy-tale cartoons, beginning with the already completed *Little Red Riding Hood*. Disney and his fellow artists plunged into their new venture with boundless youthful optimism. With the money raised by the sale of stock, the company purchased equipment, including a used 35mm Universal camera. To speed up processing (Disney had previously sent his exposed film to Chicago to be developed, which meant a delay of at least a week), Laugh-O-gram Films bought its own printing and processing equipment.

The company's gradually expanding staff included several names which would become legendary in American animation. Walt Disney was now animating alongside Hugh Harman, Lorey Tague, and Carman "Max" Maxwell. Rudy Ising did a bit of everything — drawing, operating the camera, printing and processing too. William "Red" Lyon, who had been a cameraman at Kansas City Film Ad, took on the same position at Laugh-O-grams (his business card officially claimed the title of "technical engineer"). As 1922 progressed, Otto Walliman joined the animators. The staff also included Adolph Kloepper as the business manager, Leslie Mace as a salesman, and Disney's friend Walt Pfeiffer as a "scenario editor."

Disney recruited where he could. Some of these employees, such as Lyon and Hugh

The poster for Disney's first full-story cartoon short. Spurred by his success with program fillers, in 1922 Disney produced a series of modernized fairy tales, starting with *Little Red Riding Hood*. The cartoon was animated in Disney's garage and financed by Disney's salary at the Film Ad service. (Courtesy Walt Disney Company)

A stock certificate for the newly-formed Laugh-O-gram Films, Inc., issued a month after the company incorporated on 23 May 1922. Ising paid $400 for his eight shares; a year-and-a-half later, the company was bankrupt. (Courtesy Rudy Ising)
Below: The building at 31st Street in Kansas City where Laugh-O-grams had its offices on the second floor, at far right. (Carman Maxwell Collection)

The Laugh-O-gram office in summer 1922. (Courtesy Walt Disney Company)

Walt Disney at his Laugh-O-gram drawing board. (Courtesy Walt Disney Company)

Harman, came from Kansas City Film Ad; others were attracted from elsewhere. Carman Maxwell simply happened to be walking past the building. "I was going to junior college in Kansas City and looking for some part-time work," he told Milt Gray and Mike Barrier.[1] "I saw this sign on the second-story window of a little place out at 31st and Troost in Kansas City. It said 'Laugh-O-gram Films, Inc.' I was interested in cartooning — I'd been doing a little of it during my high school and college career, for the annuals and things like that — so I went up there to investigate, and got a job."

Although the Laugh-O-gram employees were all given official titles, the division of labor was highly informal. All of them were learning a new craft and a new business together, by trial and error, and whatever needed doing was done without regard to strict job classifications. Red Lyon was designated as the company cameraman, but Rudy Ising and, occasionally, Max Maxwell also had a hand in the camera work. Maxwell described the camera setup to Gray and Barrier: "Just four four-by-fours with a table on it, and the Universal camera was mounted up above and it was connected with a little chain to a crank down one side, on one of the posts, and you just cranked every time for one turn of the camera, one frame." Maxwell recalled that he eventually found his real niche in background painting.

All the artists were young and high-spirited, and along with the work of producing the films, there was also time for youthful high jinks. At one point they decided that their camera was not impressive-looking enough for publicity shots, since it looked basically

Walt Disney and his crew promote the Laugh-O-grams in a parade of the South Central Business Association. Walt Disney is seated in the back seat, Leslie Mace has his foot on the running board, and Rudolph Ising is behind the car wearing a straw hat. (Courtesy Walt Disney Company)

like a box with a lens attached to it ("one thing about using a Universal camera," Rudy Ising pointed out, "it only had a two hundred-foot magazine"). So they painted a box to look like a camera, and nailed two film cans to the top to represent the magazine. "We used to have fun on weekends," said Ising, "going to Union Station, acting like — Walt would turn his cap around and pretend to make a film. And you know, people would come up and pose and say 'Where are you from?' And we'd say 'New York.'" The group would also shoot gag photos at Swope Park and other locations, posing with their fake camera. It was convincing enough that at least one of the photos has been reprinted in modern publications, passed off as an authentic production shot.

As summer wore on the company, slowly but methodically, continued work on its films. *The Four Musicians of Bremen* was soon completed, followed by *Jack and the Beanstalk*. Ising remembered that the latter film was marked by an important experiment with cel animation. "Walt had animated, I think it was an eight-drawing cycle of the beanstalk growing. Because I don't even think we had vertical pans then, they were all horizontal, the only way our camera would work it. So that had to be an animated thing. And for some reason the beanstalk pictures all had to be cutouts, so that the character showed behind the drawings. And they were all cut — I remember, because I did it, and then glued those onto a sheet of celluloid. In effect, it became the background. And when I was cutting those, I talked to Walt about it and said, 'Look, I don't know why we can't paint that on the cel instead of cutting that whole thing out,' because, you know, that was a lot of work, cutting around all those leaves. And after that we began using cels a little bit more and more, for animation — for cycles, especially."

Seen today, the animation of the Laugh-O-gram films sometimes has a stiff, wooden appearance. This is because the various artists, attempting to achieve a consistent appearance in each character, often simply traced the characters from Disney's model sheets. In later years this would have been regarded as cheating; in Laugh-O-gram days it was considered standard procedure. "That's what animation was," Ising confirmed, "very often you'd trace the character off of a model sheet. And that model sheet was photographed, and it was three different sizes, for close-up, medium shot or long shot. Because the camera didn't move, so you had to *draw* a closeup, and you used the bigger heads then." For expediency's sake, stock characters were devised — a boy, a girl, a bearded old man, a dog and a cat — who appeared in virtually identical form from one film to the next.

Early in November 1922, Disney hired a man who would revolutionize his studio. This was Ubbe Iwerks, his friend and former business partner. Iwerks would eventually establish himself as one of the finest animators of the Twenties, and would play a major role in Disney's earliest successes. "Ubbe was really a lettering man," Ising recalled. "He didn't do much animation to start with, but he'd do all the titles. Oh, he was a hell of a good lettering man, always with a brush. He did everything with a brush. He didn't animate with a brush, but he could have. That is where he got that beautiful swing that he had; he was great with a brush."

Another new employee, hired shortly after Iwerks, became invaluable in another way. Nadine Simpson was hired as a bookkeeper and cashier, but her singular value lay in her connections. She had previously worked at one of the Kansas City film exchanges. Knowing that the exchanges regularly junked prints when they became too worn for theatrical use, she arranged to obtain the discarded cartoons. Ising later recalled how he cut out sections of the films, particularly those showing cycles or chases, and spliced them into loops. Then the artists would look at them over and over, studying the timing of the action. Paul Terry's Aesop's Fables were the most frequent objects of this scrutiny. (This is a point worth noting, not least because of the hordes of mice that regularly appeared in Terry's cartoons. The crowds of mice in some of Disney's own subsequent films — and perhaps even the genesis of Mickey himself — may owe something to Terry's early influence.)

In these early Laugh-O-gram days, enthusiasm often overruled practicality. The films are marked by their lavish look — minutely detailed backgrounds, a full range of gray tones — and by their superabundance of gag and story ideas. The viewer gets the feeling that Disney and company, despite their inexperience, were striving to pack as much as possible into their films. The fact that the company *still* had no income seemed not to bother them at all. But by midsummer 1922 they felt ready to offer their product to the world, and their first trade advertisement — promising a series of twelve Laugh-O-grams — appeared in *Motion Picture News* in July.

When this ad failed to attract a flood of offers, Laugh-O-grams acted with characteristic extravagance. Leslie Mace, the company salesman, was sent to New York City in late summer to storm the distribution market and secure a contract. At this point, the fledgling company finally ran head-on into the hard realities of the film business. Despite all the loving detail that had been lavished on the Laugh-O-grams, Mace could find no takers. Meanwhile, his bills at the McGalpin Hotel were rapidly draining the company's meager resources.

Finally, just on the verge of returning to Kansas City in defeat, Mace met William R. Kelley, who represented the Tennessee branch of a group called Pictorial Clubs, Inc. Pictorial Clubs was a non-theatrical film distributor, dealing exclusively with schools and churches. The company also dabbled in production of its own films; a few years later it would co-produce a six-reel feature based on Bruce Barton's work of revisionist Christianity, *The Man Nobody Knows*. This was a far cry from the major theatrical distributor for which the young artists had hoped, but Kelley *was* interested in the Laugh-O-grams, and at this point Disney's chastened salesman was eager to land a contract.

Accordingly, an agreement between Laugh-O-gram Films and Pictorial Clubs was signed on 16 September 1922, for the delivery of six Laugh-O-grams. The Laugh-O-gram forces were clearly desperate by this time, and Pictorial Clubs must have appeared a savior. But the resulting agreement reinforces the impression of naive youngsters being conned by city slickers, for the contract was outrageous. The agreed-upon price seemed fair enough: $11,100 for six films, or $1850 apiece. But only $100 of that amount was specified as a down payment. Pictorial Clubs was not required to pay the $11,000 balance until 1 January 1924, 15 months later! This lengthy interval with no prospect of income would have been a crippling setback, even if the contract had been followed to the letter — but as it happened, the Tennessee branch of Pictorial Clubs went out of business shortly after the contract was signed. The New York branch acquired the assets of the Tennessee branch (including the Laugh-O-grams, all of which had been delivered by then), but was not obligated for any of its liabilities. In short, Disney and company were swindled, and their contract with Pictorial Clubs became a death grip that virtually guaranteed Laugh-O-grams' demise.

To Disney's credit, he quickly realized what a potential disaster the contract represented, and immediately took action to save his company. The bulk of its contractual obligation was already satisfied; the fourth Laugh-O-gram, *Goldie Locks and the Three Bears*, was completed, and the fifth, *Puss in Boots*, was under way. Now, even as Disney redoubled his efforts to finish *Puss in Boots* and the sixth and last in the series, *Cinderella*, he simultaneously embarked on other productions which might bring Laugh-O-grams some sorely needed income. Ultimately the little company produced an assortment of films of a remarkable range and variety.

Lafflets

Even before their brush with Pictorial Clubs, Disney and his artists had realized the importance of diversification. As early as the fall of 1921, they had started producing, in addition to the Laugh-O-grams themselves, short joke reels. "We had, usually, jokes from *Judge* and *Life* magazine," Rudy Ising later explained, "and they put a bunch of them together. And some of them had matchstick animation." These pictures were, in essence, a continuation of the former Newman Laugh-O-grams, but in order to distinguish them from the company's more ambitious efforts they were dubbed Lafflets. Originally the artists produced them just for fun, and for the opportunity to experiment.

In the wake of the Pictorial Clubs contract, however, Disney looked to the Lafflets for a source of income that might help to tide the company over. In mid-November Aletha Reynolds was hired, partly as an inker and painter, but also specifically for editorial work on the Lafflets. Disney's thinking was rather daring, even reckless: faced with financial ruin, he hired yet another employee. Still, if a market could have been found for the Lafflets, they *would* have made an ideal stopgap. They could be produced quickly and easily, and had a built-in novelty appeal. Further, their loose format allowed for experimentation with a wide range of techniques. (Some of them included clay modeling, juxtaposed with cel and matchstick animation.) By March of 1923 a sample reel was ready to be sent to Universal. Acceptance by such a major company, even on modest terms, would have given Laugh-O-grams a new lease on life. But Universal was not interested.

Apparently none of the Lafflets survive, but Rudy Ising's memories of them make them sound intriguing. He remembered one in which Ubbe Iwerks appeared, walking up to a formless mass of clay and working furiously (like the sketching hand in the Newman reels) to produce a clay model of Warren G. Harding. Then Iwerks walked away, leaving Harding smoking a cigarette. "The model was made, complete. And then what happened is that he walked in backwards; everything was shot in reverse. He walked in backwards, but actually, when you ran it, he was walking away. He walked in to the clay model, turned around and started just really throwing this clay. I think we did a slow crank on that [to speed up the action on screen]. And then when it was over, then we cut to the closeups with the smoke coming from the cigarette and whatnot."

Tommy Tucker's Tooth

One Laugh-O-gram project that did bring in some cash was an educational film commissioned by a local dentist. Dr. Thomas B. McCrum, whose offices were at the Deaner Dental Institute, offered Disney $500 to produce a film which might be shown to school children to teach them dental care. Disney quickly accepted the offer. It was agreed that the film would be largely a live-action production, featuring a cast of local children. (Live action was, as always, faster and cheaper to produce than animation. Disney, looking ahead, had purchased a used tripod in September 1922 to facilitate live-action shooting.)

Tommy Tucker's Tooth contrasts virtuous Tommy Tucker, who takes good care of his teeth and keeps up his general appearance, with the unruly Jimmie Jones, forever negligent and unkempt. Both apply to the same company for a job; Tommy, because of his neat appearance, is hired immediately, while Jimmie is refused — until he changes his ways. Disney held auditions at various Kansas City schools to recruit his cast, and from Thomas H. Benton Elementary School, which Disney himself had attended, came an 11-year-old boy named Jack Records to play the role of Jimmie Jones.

John W. Records, who would go on to a distinguished medical career, retained fond memories of his experience working in the film. He laughed that he enjoyed it simply because he was excused from school for the filming: "At that point, age eleven, I wasn't the most avid student in the world." Walt Disney as a director made a strong impression on him. "I don't recall any script — if he had a script, I didn't see it — but he always knew exactly what he wanted us to do. And he would act things out. I can't think of any specifics, but I do have a very strong recollection of how organized and prepared he was. It was all very informal — I mean, he liked children, it was obvious, and he knew how to handle us. I was impressed with that too, because the way he did it, why, it was fun." In later years the film held a private irony for Dr. Records: "I never had any idea, as I was doing this, what a career I would have as a patient of dentists." Filmed in December 1922, *Tommy Tucker's Tooth* remained in circulation long after its production; ten years later, Dr. Records' fiancee saw it in a university home nursing class.

This little film, Disney's first educational production, has a particular significance in the overall context of his career. In later years he would be celebrated for his ability to inform or instruct through film, and in *Tommy Tucker's Tooth* we can see that gift in embryo. The explanation of concepts by simple, easily-understood illustrations would become a hallmark of Disney's later educational films. Here we can already see that idea at work, as Disney correlates dental-care principles with the need to refrigerate food to prevent spoilage, or to darn holes in socks to keep them from growing larger. (In this connection it would be fascinating to know more about Dr. McCrum's involvement with the film; if he did, as the credit title suggests, write the story, he can be credited with an important and unsung influence on Disney's career.) Dr. Records had a personal illustration of the film's effectiveness when he ran his print (made for him in later years by the Disney company) for one of his grandchildren. "His mother told me the next day that she could hardly get him to go to bed, because that night he stood in the bathroom and practiced brushing his teeth!"

Martha

Meanwhile, the pressing need for cash produced yet another line of shorts tied to local business. This was a proposed series of illustrated sing-along films, the audience participation novelty that had been popular since the birth of the nickelodeon. Preserving the format of the company name, the song films were dubbed Song-O-Reels, and they grew out of an agreement between Disney, a Kansas City music publisher called the Jenkins Music Company, and the Isis Theater. But like the Lafflets, the project quickly failed. Only one Song-O-Reel was produced, to illustrate Jenkins' recently published ballad "Martha: Just a Plain Old Fashioned Name," by Joe L. Sanders. The film, now lost, is of interest today largely because it brought Disney into contact with another vital collaborator in his later films. Carl Stalling, the Isis organist, had already achieved a

Filming the live-action Song-O-Reel *Martha.* Left: Disney as director and Ubbe Iwerks as the love-sick hero; assisting Disney is business manager Adolph Kloepper. Right: Disney is in the director's chair, Rudolph Ising is on the stool, Walt Pfeiffer is kneeling in the background, and Red Lyon is behind the camera. Bottom: Title card for the Song-O-Reel *Martha.* (Courtesy Walt Disney Company)

measure of local fame. He would later be lured to Hollywood, where he would begin his celebrated animation career by writing music for Disney's early Mickey Mouse and Silly Symphony cartoons.

The only surviving remnants of *Martha* are a handful of stills, a title card designed by Ubbe Iwerks, and eyewitness accounts. These indicate that the film was largely or entirely live-action, shot in homemade sets and scenic Kansas City locations, and that Iwerks once again was featured on screen. The title card is designed with the same level of care and detail as were the Laugh-O-grams; Disney was clearly hoping to release the film on far more than a local basis.

Alice's Wonderland

By far the most significant of these "alternative" Laugh-O-gram productions, and perhaps the most significant of all Disney's Kansas City films, took shape in the spring of 1923. Disney, in his constant search for new and different film ideas, had a sudden inspiration. Even before his new project was well under way, he was writing to potential

Carl Stalling, later Disney's music director, was already well-known locally as a top-flight organist at the Isis movie theater. *The Kansas City Star*, 26 Feb 1922.
Right: Walt Disney and Virginia Davis watch the animation board in the first Alice, *Alice's Wonderland*. (Courtesy Walt Disney Company)

distributors with genuine enthusiasm: "We have just discovered something new and clever in animated cartoons!"[2]

The new discovery was actually a reversal of a device which had been common for some time: the combination of live action and animation. Numerous films had already shown animated characters escaping the confines of their cartoon settings and entering the real world; this was, for one example, a staple of the Fleischer brothers' Out of the Inkwell series. Disney's twist was to reverse the process, to show a *live* character entering a *cartoon* world. The result was *Alice's Wonderland*, in which a little girl, her imagination excited by a visit to a cartoon studio, dreamed of a trip aboard an animated train to Cartoonland.

The role of Alice was taken by a four-year-old girl named Virginia Davis, who had already made a local name for herself as a child model and performer. She had, in fact, been employed by Kansas City Film Ad, and Disney first saw her in one of their advertisements for Warneker's Bread. "It was just a picture of me," Virginia later recalled, "smiling and looking like 'Oh, yum yum!' and eating this piece of Warneker's Bread with a lot of jam on it." Disney contacted Virginia's parents and negotiated a contract for her appearance in the film. The contract, guaranteeing Virginia 5% of Laugh-O-grams' receipts from *Alice's Wonderland*, was signed on 13 April 1923.

Aware that this film might be his last chance, Disney plunged into it in an all-or-nothing gamble. No resource of his studio was spared. An elaborate script was prepared, flaunting the most stunning trick effects the artists could devise. Some of Alice's dream scenes were so intricate that they could be achieved only by making still photographs of

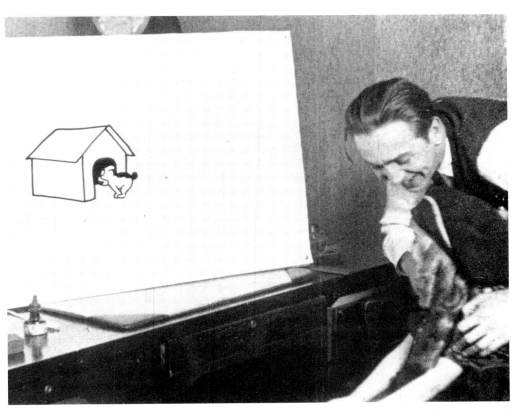

the little girl, and "animating" them alongside the drawings. Other scenes featured such embellishments as a live-action cat harassed by an animated mouse with a sword. (The main title proudly proclaimed that these scenes were "produced by a Laugh-O-gram process.")

The finished film showed clearly the effort that had gone into it; if the fairy-tale cartoons had been lavish, *Alice's Wonderland* was downright extravagant. The dream scene in Cartoonland emerged as a charming, ornately detailed fantasy. The cartoon studio scenes preserved an historic glimpse of the interior of the Laugh-O-grams studio, not to mention performances by Walt Disney and other staff members. Disney showed the same instinct that he would show so many years later with *Snow White and the Seven Dwarfs*: faced with economic hardship, he responded, not with economy measures, but with the most memorably sumptuous film he could make.

It is tantalizing to speculate on what might have happened had one of these supplemental projects borne fruit, or had Disney's distributor proven solvent and honest. If Universal had accepted the Lafflets, or if *Martha* had caught on and inaugurated a series of Song-O-Reels, or if Pictorial Clubs had paid even a part of their debt in advance, Laugh-O-gram Films might have survived — altering subsequent film history in ways that can only be imagined.

But Disney's resourcefulness was not limited to developing supplemental film series; he was also adept at enlisting new investors as the company resources tapered off. Between October 1922 and June 1923, Laugh-O-gram Films tried to cover its debts with substantial loans from two would-be investors. These were Dr. John V. Cowles, a local surgeon, and J. Fred Schmeltz, who owned a hardware store. Schmeltz, a particularly canny businessman, secured each of his loans with chattel mortgages on Laugh-O-grams' assets. By June 1923 he was, at least on paper, the owner of all the company's equipment *and* the Pictorial Clubs contract![3] Meanwhile, Laugh-O-grams was resorting to more and more economy measures, including a move in summer 1923 to less expensive quarters in the nearby Wirthman Building.

Trying to keep his debt-ridden company afloat was a seemingly futile exercise, but Disney's efforts in another area were about to pay off. In May 1923, his volley of letters to potential distributors brought a reply from M. J. Winkler. Though *Alice's Wonderland* was still far from complete, Disney continued to court Winkler's interest as energetically as he could.

This correspondence was itself an indicator of Disney's unflagging optimism, for Margaret J. Winkler was no ordinary distributor. On the contrary, she represented the pinnacle of the American animation business at the time, being the distributor of Pat Sullivan's enormously popular Felix the Cat cartoons and, for the time being, of the Fleischer brothers' Out of the Inkwell series. She was, indeed, largely responsible for the success of the Felix films; she had taken on the series at a time when it was relatively little-known and, through her aggressive promotion and publicity, achieved an unprecedented level of success for both Felix and herself. A Winkler release for Laugh-O-grams' films would virtually guarantee their success.

But that hope alone was not enough to sustain the company for long, especially when *Alice's Wonderland*, the object of Winkler's interest, was not finished until August. By that time Laugh-O-gram Films' staggering debts, combined with the lack of any definite prospects for the future, had become impossible to ignore. The company's days were clearly numbered. Disney was optimistic, but not stupid, and he now decided that his only chance for success was to leave Kansas City and move to one of the film production centers.

That he would ultimately choose Hollywood seems a foregone conclusion today, but in 1923, virtually all of the American animation industry was centered in New York City. The determining factor in Disney's decision to move to California appears to have been his older brother Roy, who had been wounded in the war and was now recuperating in the veterans' hospital in Sawtelle. Roy was convinced that, with Walt's ideas and experience and his own business sense, they might successfully produce films together. He wrote encouraging letters to Walt, urging him to come out and pointing out that he could stay with their Uncle Robert, who owned a house on Kingswell Avenue in Hollywood.

During these declining months, with its theatrical productions bringing in only a meager return, Laugh-O-gram Films had survived by other means. Disney and Red Lyon made use of the company's camera by working as occasional stringers for the Pathé and

Young Disney behind the camera. (Courtesy Walt Disney Company)

Universal newsreels, recording any newsworthy events in Kansas City. Another side venture, inaugurated the previous fall, was the making of professional "home movies" for the proud parents of young children. This service included both the filming of the child and home showings of the film, but Lyon explained to the *Kansas City Star* in October 1922 that in the future everyone would have a projector and the home showings would be unnecessary.

This service was a humbling extremity for one who had grand ambitions as a filmmaker, but it did produce some much-needed income. And there is general agreement that one of these baby-filming jobs, late in the summer of 1923, provided Disney with the funds he needed to make his move to California. In more than one interview of the 1930s, Disney acknowledged that his trip was financed by such a film, made for a doctor whose offices were near the now nearly-deserted Laugh-O-gram studio. (This bit of good fortune would later backfire on Disney in an unexpected way. When, having achieved worldwide fame, he returned to Kansas City in 1936 to receive an award, he was contacted by the same doctor — who wanted Disney's help in getting his now considerably older child into the movies!)

And so, in August 1923, Walt Disney left Kansas City for California, carrying little more than a small amount of money ($40, according to most accounts) and a print of *Alice's Wonderland*. The rights to the film still belonged to Laugh-O-grams, which was heavily in debt, but Disney had visions of a whole series of Alice films, and obtained permission from his creditors to use this first effort as a sample reel.

At this time the due date for Pictorial Clubs' $11,000 payment was only five months away, but subsequent events were to confirm Disney's foresight in leaving when he did. The Tennessee branch of Pictorial Clubs, with which Laugh-O-grams had contracted, was long since defunct. The New York branch had acquired all its assets, including the Laugh-O-grams, but had no intention of paying its debts. Bankruptcy proceedings for Laugh-O-gram Films were instituted in October 1923, and only after three and a half

After Disney went bankrupt, Harman, Ising, and Maxwell started their own Arabian Nights animation studio, purchasing their equipment and furniture from defunct Laugh-O-gram. (Courtesy Rudy Ising)

years of harassment by an aggressive legal firm was the money extracted from Pictorial Clubs. By that time, of course, Disney was firmly established in Hollywood.

In the meantime, Hugh Harman, Rudy Ising and Max Maxwell, still bitten by the animation bug, decided to see whether they could succeed where Laugh-O-grams had failed. Fred Schmeltz was now the legal owner of the Laugh-O-grams equipment, and Harman, Ising and Maxwell approached him early in the fall of 1923 and arranged to buy some of it. Armed with the Universal camera and its stand, two animating booths, and miscellaneous other equipment from the failed company, they tentatively launched a studio of their own under the name "Arabian Nights." A trial film was produced, and the trio tried to market it, but were no more successful than Laugh-O-grams had been.

The Arabian Nights studio also produced a notable experiment: a song reel which was a sort of follow-up to *Martha*. For this effort Carl Stalling chose the song "When You Come to the End of a Perfect Day," and, as Rudy Ising remembered it, also devised a homemade method of synchronization. Before the three artists started production of the film, they accompanied Stalling to the projection booth of the Isis Theater. There the Isis projectionist hand-cranked a discarded reel of film through the projector, while Stalling traced a stationary pencil along the surface of the film. "And Carl, with the pencil, just literally pressed the film each time," Ising explained. "And from that we could tell exactly where the words came and how long they were held — 'day' would be held, maybe, for so many frames. And from that we made the exposure sheets." These in turn were used to time the appearances of the lyrics on screen. "And then Carl played to it, and the guy projected it at exactly the same speed, so he knew exactly what was going to happen."

Stalling's interest in the combination of music and film would find a significant outlet in later years. And he, Harman, Ising, and Maxwell — along with some of the other Laugh-O-gram veterans — would all cross paths with Walt Disney again. Collectively, building on their Kansas City apprenticeship, they would produce a body of films that would make history.

Notes

1. Interview with Milt Gray, 1977. Courtesy of Mike Barrier.
2. Letter from Disney to Winkler, 5/14/23.
3. Cowles' connection with Laugh-O-grams apparently began in October 1922 with Leslie Mace's attempts to collect his back salary. After some negotiations Cowles advanced the company $2500 on 30 November, and over the next few months his total investment was increased to $3700. Schmeltz's first loan was made in February 1923, followed by two more in June, each secured by a separate chattel mortgage. Later, during bankruptcy proceedings against Laugh-O-grams, Schmeltz tried to use these securities to claim priority over the other creditors — an attempt which was unsuccessful. Laugh-O-gram bankruptcy papers courtesy National Archives, Central Plains Region.

ALICE COMEDIES

When Walt Disney arrived in Los Angeles in August 1923, he was anything but discouraged. Indeed, he seemed inspired by the failure of the Kansas City venture; he was now in the filmmaking capital of the world, and he was ready to make films. One of his first acts upon arrival was to buy a Pathé camera, for $200, from John W. Peterson of Peterson's Camera Exchange. He also began making the rounds of potential distributors, carrying a print of *Alice's Wonderland*. And he was careful to maintain his correspondence with Margaret Winkler, hoping to cultivate the interest she had already shown.

This correspondence was a delicate matter, for Disney was anxious to put the best possible face on his impoverished circumstances. His letters were confident and polished, typed on an impressive new letterhead. No mention was made of the Laugh-O-grams bankruptcy; Disney told Winkler only that he had moved to the coast to take advantage of the better facilities and more experienced talent there. This, of course, was perfectly true as far as it went, but Winkler wanted to see more than letters. "We have been corresponding with each other since your first letter to me of May 14th," she wrote to Disney in September. "It seems to me that this is about all it has amounted to." Clearly, it was time to let her see *Alice's Wonderland*.

As it happened, Disney had the unexpected advantage of good timing. Margaret Winkler was, as we have mentioned, the distributor of Pat Sullivan's Felix the Cat series, the most popular and most prestigious cartoon series on the market. Had Disney, an unproven beginner, written her a year earlier, she might well have ignored his overtures. Early in September 1923, however, she became embroiled in a contract dispute with Pat Sullivan, and for a good nine months her distributorship of the Felix series was in question. Coincidentally or not, it was shortly afterward, in mid-October, that Disney received a telegram from her. She had seen *Alice's Wonderland*, was guardedly enthusiastic about it, and offered Disney a contract. Disney had found a distributor; he signed the contract on 16 October 1923.[1] His situation was now the exact reverse of his previous dilemma in Kansas City: he had a distributor, but no studio, no staff, and no films. (Even *Alice's Wonderland* could be used only as a sample. Caught up in the Laugh-O-gram bankruptcy proceedings, it was off-limits for public exhibition.) Winkler's terms called for twelve films, and offered Disney $1500 for each of the first six, after which she could either exercise or drop her option for the remaining six. The first title was to be delivered by the 15th of December, two months away. Walt and Roy Disney went to work.

Their new studio was a tiny office which they had rented a week before receiving the Winkler telegram. It was located in the rear of a building occupied by the Holly-Vermont Realty company at 4651 Kingswell Avenue, two blocks away from Uncle Robert's house. The rent was all of $10 per month. The question of where to shoot the live-action portions of the films was, for the time being, unresolved. The Disneys considered renting

Walt.Disney
Cartoonist

4406 KINGSWELL
LOS ANGELES

Oct 24 1923

Dear Mrs Davis

I wired you last night for still photos of Virginia which will be used for Publicity and advertising —

In my last letter to you I said that final signing of contracts had not been completed — However everything is complete now and my proposition to you can be put in force.

However before I can go ahead and do any work in the publicity line it will be necessary for me to have a letter from you accepting my proposition and later when you come out we can sign contracts —. You can plan on being here by Nov 15 ready to start work — I am already working on the first picture. — please send letter of acceptance at once — awaiting your reply I am

yours truly Walt Disney

P.S. In your letter of acceptance — repeat the terms I stated —

space at one of several studios in the area, but ultimately abandoned this plan as too expensive.

Next, they went after Alice. Winkler's contract specified that the Alice of the new series must be played by the same girl who had appeared in *Alice's Wonderland.* Accordingly, on 16 October Disney wrote to Virginia Davis' mother in Kansas City, offering a year's contract for Virginia's services. Almost immediately the Davis family wired back, agreeing to move to California. This may seem surprising, since the Alice series was still such a speculative venture, but even at this early date Disney was a master salesman. "It would be a big opportunity for [Virginia]," he wrote, "and would introduce her to the profession in a manner that few children could receive."[2] In another letter he pointed out: "It is an opportunity that is hard to get on account of the great number of mothers that want to place their children in the movies."

The Davises were also motivated by other influences, as Virginia later explained: "I think it was a combination of factors. First of all, I'd had a very bad bout of pneumonia and almost died, and the doctor said it would be good in dry country. And my dad was a traveling salesman; he was a furniture salesman and he took out samples. And I think they decided, well, why stay here, we can go there and have the dry country and Gini can do this, and so forth."

Upon receipt of Margaret Davis' telegram, Disney quickly wrote again outlining his terms. Virginia was to receive an escalating monthly salary, beginning at $100 and rising to $200 by the end of the year, with an option on her further services at $250 per month. He added that he and his brother would need to have Virginia available by mid-November. In a further letter on 24 October, he indicated that he was already at work on the animation of the first picture. The Davises happily accepted his terms and proceeded with their move to Hollywood.

In the meantime Disney had taken the precaution of inquiring into Margaret Winkler's background and requesting a confidential bank report on her. The responses were positive, confirming that she was a solid, reputable businesswoman. On 24 October Disney wrote to her, agreeing to meet the 15 December deadline, and informing her that the first entry in the series would be *Alice's Day at Sea.* Production was already under way.

Thus were launched the Alice Comedies, Disney's first full-fledged series of films. This series ran for three and a half years, and marked a major turning point in Disney's career. In that time he graduated from ambitious beginner to experienced producer, with a studio and staff capable of producing animated films that rivaled the best in the business. Speaking of his studio in later years, Disney was fond of saying that "it all started with a mouse" — but in fact the foundation was laid in 1924 by a little girl.

Disney and Virginia Davis flanked by two fisherman on location in Santa Monica for *Alice's Day at Sea.* At far right, Virginia's parents.
Overleaf: Generic lobby card for the first Alice series. Disney reversed the formula of Max Fleischer's Out of the Inkwell series, putting live-action Alice in an animated setting.
(Courtesy Virginia Davis McGhee)
Copyright registration of the Alice Comedy trademark.

It makes a good story — as reported by a magazine writer in 1934,[3] and repeated in nearly every published account since then — that the new series was called "Alice in Cartoonland." It would have been an imaginative title, and a fitting one. But all the evidence indicates that no one thought of it at the time. Title cards of the surviving films, production papers, trade reviews, copyright records, publicity materials, all confirm that the series was never identified by any group title but Alice Comedies or, simply, Alice.

The series got off to a bumpy start — not surprisingly, for, by contrast with the reckless extravagance of the Kansas City days, Walt and Roy Disney were operating with a bare minimum of resources. The new company was christened the "Disney Bros. Studio," and its first two films were, indeed, produced by the two brothers alone. Walt in particular was carrying a heavy burden, for he was the studio's only artist. Whereas the animation and backgrounds of *Alice's Wonderland* had been the combined work of seven artists, Walt Disney wrote, designed and animated *Alice's Day at Sea* singlehanded.

Along with the artwork, Walt directed the live-action scenes, while Roy, the business manager, doubled as company cameraman, photographing both the animation and the live action. Live-action scenes, being much easier and less time-consuming to produce than animation, were highly important to the early Alices. The casts, aside from Virginia Davis, were recruited from the ranks of neighborhood children; the Disneys would devise framing stories for them to act out. One of those children was Ruthie Tompson, who lived on Kingswell Avenue — and who would, coincidentally, enjoy a long and active career at the Disney studio in later years. In later years she said of Virginia Davis: "I hated her! Wouldn't you be jealous of a little girl, yes you would, I mean if you were a little girl and this little kid came with all her little bouncing curls and everything? Cute little girl. She was getting all the attention." On the other hand, Ruthie liked Roy Disney very much, and would stop at the studio on her way home from school to watch him shoot the animation. "I remember how that funny light made my fingernails turn purple."

Alice's Day at Sea arrived at Winkler's New York office on 26 December, eleven days over schedule. Immediately Disney received a telegram asking him to ship all of his positive and negative raw footage. "We believe same can possibly be improved by re-editing here," Winkler told him, adding gently, "All our films are recut in New York." Even after recutting, the film was something of a disappointment to Winkler. "I would suggest you inject as much humor as you possibly can," she wrote Disney in January. She also asked him to sell her the negative of *Alice's Wonderland* outright, "as emergency backup against future uncertainties." (This of course was impossible, for Disney was no longer the legal owner of the film — a fact which he, in his eagerness to make a good impression, had failed to mention. This oversight would later contribute to an atmosphere of distrust between the two parties.)

The second film, *Alice Hunting in Africa,* arrived at Winkler's office at the end of January and elicited a similar response. This time Winkler acknowledged an improvement in the timing of the film, but still felt the element of humor was lacking. Regarding the comedy in the picture, she wrote: "Please again let me impress on you that future productions must be of a much higher standard than those we have already seen." Such comments were Disney's introduction to the true nature of his relationship with the Winkler company. Margaret Winkler and her staff seemed to regard him not as a business associate, but as a child who must be taken in hand and taught the rudiments of editing, laboratory work, and even story construction. This may seem ludicrous in light of Disney's later success, but for the time being Disney seemed grateful for their comments, and continued to send them the raw footage of each Alice Comedy. If his filmmaking education began with E. G. Lutz, it entered a new phase with M. J. Winkler.

The framing stories of the early Alices, with their continuing casts of children, sometimes bore more than a faint resemblance to the Our Gang comedies of Hal Roach. Disney seemed unconcerned about this at first, and even cultivated the resemblance in such films as *Alice and the Dog Catcher.* Some of his regular cast members, too, seemed to be chosen with an eye on Roach's troupe. Freckle-faced Spec O'Donnell, soon to achieve fame on his own, made an effective counterpart to Roach regular Mickey Daniels; Our Gang's Fat Joe Cobb found a Disney parallel in Leon Holmes; and Roach's token girl, Mary Kornman, was of course balanced by Virginia Davis herself. And special mention should be made of Peggy, a German shepherd owned by Disney's Uncle Robert, who was more than a match for the Gang's famous dog, Pete. Disney did not hesitate to exploit Peggy's talent, and she appeared in his films as late as 1926.

Meanwhile, the Disney brothers were receiving some much-needed relief as their staff began to expand. To begin with, two girls were hired to ink and paint the cels. One of them, a dark-haired beauty named Lillian Bounds, doubled as a secretary. A romance soon blossomed between Walt and Lillian, leading to their marriage in July 1925. Another important addition was Rollin C. "Ham" Hamilton, who signed on in February to assist Walt with the animation. He would remain a prominent part of the studio's animation staff throughout most of the silent period, and continued his career elsewhere in later years.

In order to accommodate the increasing size of their staff, the Disneys moved from their tiny quarters to the vacant store next door at 4649 Kingswell, and also rented a separate garage. These new facilities supplemented a vacant lot at Hollywood Boulevard and Rodney Drive which the Disneys had rented in January, during production of *Alice Hunting in Africa.* This served as an open-air stage for the shooting of the live-action scenes. A large white canvas drop was put up behind a billboard that faced the Boulevard, and used for Virginia Davis' scenes which were to be combined with animation. (Wrinkles in the drop are sometimes discernible in the early Alices.) With his new personnel and new facilities, Disney was hoping for shorter production time on his third film, *Alice's Spooky Adventure.* Unfortunately, shooting of the live-action scenes was hampered by incessant clouds and fog, and the film was not completed and shipped until the 22nd of February.

Nevertheless, an improvement was immediately apparent. Upon receiving *Alice's*

Filming *Alice's Spooky Adventure.*
Below: The makeshift outdoor set
for the finale of *Alice's Spooky
Adventure.* Walt Disney (left) directs
Virginia and Roy Disney shoots
while Davis' father looks on.
(Courtesy Virginia Davis McGhee)
Opposite: Posing Virginia Davis in
front of the white screen for the
photographs to be "animated" along
with the drawings in *Alice the
Peacemaker.* (Courtesy Walt Disney
Company)

Alice hauled off to jail in an unused scene from *Alice's Spooky Adventure*.
Below: Little Virginia responds to peer criticism from Leon Holmes in *Alice's Wild West Show*. (Courtesy Virginia Davis McGhee)

Little Virginia and the boys (Tommy Hicks second from left) belly up to the bar in *Alice's Wild West Show*.
Below: Publicity still for *Alice's Wild West Show*.
Overleaf: Virginia Davis poses for *Alice's Wild West Show*.
(Courtesy Virginia Davis McGhee)

Frame enlargements from *Alice's Spooky Adventure* (top), *Alice's Wild West Show*, and *Alice's Fishy Story*. (Courtesy Nederlands Filmmuseum)

Spooky Adventure, Margaret Winkler quickly wrote to express her enthusiasm: "I will be frank with you and say that I have been waiting for just such a picture as 'Alice's Spooky Adventure' before using every effort to place it in all the territories throughout the world." The only deterrent was that some of the combination scenes (combining Alice with cartoon figures) were technically unsatisfactory, and Winkler returned them to Disney and asked to have them retaken. Meanwhile, an encouraged Disney plunged ahead with production of *Alice's Wild West Show*.

Even in these early days, when the live-action content of the Alices was at its height, it took far less time to photograph Virginia Davis' scenes than it did to animate the cartoon material. But Virginia's duties did not end with the making of the films; she also made personal appearances at local theaters that were showing them. Here, again, her early dancing lessons paid off. "It would be Little Virginia Davis appearing in person," she recalled, "such-and-such a date, and then they'd have the picture underneath it and so forth. They would just introduce me, and then I did a dance and took a bow and that was it." She relates a story, from one such appearance, that her mother told her in later years: "They had an orchestra, and someplace along the line they repeated my music, and she was panicky outside when she heard the music being repeated. So I just did the whole thing over again. And I came off the stage, and in baby talk — I didn't talk very well for a long time — I said to my mom: 'They 'peat my music so I 'peat my dance!'"

Interestingly, she had no memory of simply *watching* the films in a theater — or of having any desire to do so. "I didn't care," she said. "It didn't mean anything to me, because I was just doing whatever I was told to do. Kids don't care that much, you know, they're not that vain. I had fun doing it, and that was it."

As Disney continued to refine his product, Margaret Winkler became increasingly free with suggestions and well-intentioned criticism. Disney continued to accept these comments graciously, but he was quickly developing his own ideas as to the content and style of his films. As early as February he politely explained: "I am trying to comply with your instructions by injecting as much humor as possible .... It is my desire to be a little different from the usual run of slap stick and hold [the films] more to a dignified line of comedy." This was an early manifestation of the desire for refinement which would be evident throughout Disney's career.

One Winkler suggestion which was to have far-reaching results involved a cartoon sidekick for Alice. The black cat who appears in nearly all the Alices invariably reminds viewers of Felix, and this seeming plagiarism has sometimes been seen as an unfortunate reflection on Disney. In fact, however, more than one witness has confirmed that the idea for such a character actually came from Margaret Winkler herself. (Through hindsight, it seems quite likely that she saw it as a form of leverage to help keep the recalcitrant Pat Sullivan in check.) The cartoon cat in *Alice's Spooky Adventure* can easily be justified as a dream manifestation of the black cat Alice encounters in the abandoned house. The next film, *Alice's Wild West Show*, has no such justification — and when a sidekick for Alice does materialize (more than halfway through the film), he is not a black cat but a white dog! When Winkler saw this film, she quickly wrote to Disney: "I might suggest that in your cartoon stuff you use a cat wherever possible and don't be afraid to let him do ridiculous things." In the next film, *Alice's Fishy Story*, the cat obediently reappeared, but Disney remained uneasy about the character's resemblance to Felix. It was not until late in 1924 that Disney's cat evolved into the familiar figure of Julius who was to dominate the balance of the series.

Disney's own ideas for improving the series mainly revolved around improvements in the animation, and he knew just the man who could effect those improvements: Ubbe Iwerks. Iwerks was still in Kansas City, having returned to his old job at United Film Ad (as Kansas City Film Ad had been renamed). Early in the year Disney began corresponding with him, appealing to him to move to California and join the staff of the new studio. Ultimately Disney's persistence paid off, and Iwerks agreed to the move. By a happy coincidence, Thomas Davis, Virginia's father, was looking for someone to drive his Cadillac out to the coast (the Davis family had prudently made their original trip by train). It was arranged that Iwerks would deliver the car, Davis paying all his expenses. Iwerks arrived late in July 1924, and immediately there was a dramatic improvement in the animation of the Alice films. Throughout the rest of the silent years, no matter how many animators were added to Disney's animation department, Iwerks would remain the strong foundation on which the studio depended.

(Meanwhile, the Davis family's car was to play an important part in Walt Disney's personal life. He had by this time begun seriously to court Lillian, and the Davis car made it possible for him to take her out. "Well, he didn't have a car," Virginia explains, "and he would ask Mom if he could borrow the car. And she always loved him. I mean, she was very fond of Walt.")

As the stories and the animation of the series continued to improve, the one remaining liability, the live-action scenes, became an increasing irritant to all concerned. The scenes that combined live action with animation were especially critical; some entries in the series were greeted by complaints that Alice was too light and noticeably grainy in her scenes with the cartoon characters, and that those scenes were afflicted with jitters. The Disneys changed labs in an effort to improve the steadiness of the double-printed combination scenes, but the key to Alice's lightness and graininess lay elsewhere.

Inserting little Alice into an otherwise all-cartoon scene was a greater technical challenge, in this case, than it would have been to reverse the procedure and put an animated character into the real world. Other producers, such as the Fleischers, had already achieved that effect simply by blowing up a photograph, using it as their background, and photographing the cels in register with it. Disney's twist on the gimmick, on the other hand, required that most of the actual combinations be made at the printing stage. Ideally, this called for a traveling-matte process, so that the live and animated elements would not "bleed" through each other on screen.

Just how the Disneys accomplished this in 1924 is not positively known. The most commonly used traveling-matte process in the industry at that time was the Williams process (which involved the photographic generation of a high-contrast matte from the original shot), but it seems unlikely that the Disneys, in their precarious financial circumstances, would have used so complicated and expensive a method. It seems far more likely that they developed at this time the technique which Rudy Ising found in use when he arrived at the studio in mid-1925. As he recalled it, Alice's live-action scenes would be filmed first, and the desired take would be selected and printed. "And that would be put in the [animation] camera, and they had a light that went inside the camera and projected down onto a field. And then you traced the girl, the area on each frame of film, you traced it. Now those were never used in animation; in the final picture the girl was alive. But from that tracing we had to make what they called a traveling matte — they were filled in black on the white paper. And we shot that and got a negative made, and that was bi-packed in the camera when we shot the animation. And it was black around her, and then the white part of her was matted out. And then when it was printed, it was double-printed, just in reverse. You used the traveling matte with the animation negative, and then you used the reverse when you double-printed her in." However complicated this may sound, it was simpler — for an animation studio — and cheaper than the Williams process.

Rudy Ising, 1992.

This technique, or something like it, was applied in remaking the unsatisfactory scenes from *Alice's Spooky Adventure*, and was used throughout the combination scenes in *Alice's Wild West Show*, creating some of the most convincing effects in the whole series. But in a number of subsequent Alices, the live-action elements are, quite plainly, simply double-exposed over the animation. We can only speculate that Disney — who was already hard-pressed to meet his deadlines, with the studio's limited staff — decided he could not indulge in the time-consuming luxury of a matte process, and was trying to get by without it. Virginia's actions were photographed against a white drop, and the finished scenes were staged so that she appeared in an open white area. This meant that there was no contact between the live and animated portions of the scene, so that a matte would have been unnecessary — except that the white background itself showed through

One of the early technical problems Disney had to overcome: in combination scenes, Alice frequently registered too light. Here is an example from *Alice Gets in Dutch*. Below: For a short time, Disney animated Alice with photograph cut-outs. In such films, a photograph of Virginia Davis was glued onto each cel and coordinated with the drawing. This is an example from *Alice the Peacemaker*. (Courtesy Nederlands Filmmuseum)

Alice's body! This was the cause of the "lightness" that Winkler and the exhibitors were complaining about. There are signs that Disney tried to compensate for that lightness by reducing the exposure of both the live and animated elements, but this only resulted in an overall scene that was unacceptably dark. Throughout the summer and early fall of 1924 the experiments continued — and so did the complaints.

One remedy for the live-action problem was to change cameramen; it had quickly become apparent that Roy Disney's skill behind the camera was no match for his business abilities. "He never could master the cranking rhythm a cameraman must learn," Walt Disney would later tell his daughter Diane. "As a result, we ended up with a fluctuating tempo on the screen, so finally I had to hire a real cameraman and that did cost more money."[4] The real cameraman was Harry Forbes, who had earlier photographed features for Fox and Bluebird (where he had worked with Rex Ingram, among other directors). For most of the mid- to late-1924 Alices, the live-action scenes were photographed by Forbes. Roy Disney was also exempted from photographing the animation when the company hired Mike Marcus in May 1924. This work was done with the Pathé camera which Walt had purchased on his arrival in California. The Pathé had immediately been adapted for single-frame photography, and was now used exclusively for photographing the animation; the usual practice for photographing the live-action scenes was simply to rent a standard Bell and Howell camera for a day or two.

The most challenging scenes in the Alice films, from a technical standpoint, were those which involved the closest interaction between Alice and the cartoon characters. For the trickiest such scenes, Disney employed the same method he had used in *Alice's Wonderland*: a cutout photograph of Virginia, "animated" along with the cartoon characters. This method had mixed results. For the long scenes of Alice running and riding the bull's back in *Alice the Peacemaker*, the results were plainly unsatisfactory. Whether because of the glossy finish of the photographs, bad placement of the lights, or some other reason, the cutouts were so obvious as to lose their effectiveness. In *Alice's*

Wild West Show and *Alice Cans the Cannibals*, on the other hand, the same technique was used more subtly to show Virginia taking long falls that might have killed her in real life, then bouncing to her feet unhurt. These scenes work so well that they suggest further possibilities which might have been explored, if the technique had been developed. Instead it was abandoned after the first season. From then on, whenever Alice's involvement in the cartoon action became too complicated, she was simply drawn and animated along with Julius and the other characters.

As the year 1924 progressed, more and more technical refinements were added to the Alices. The multi-talented Ubbe Iwerks built a homemade motor drive for the Pathé camera, operated by a telegraph key, which made for more consistent exposure of the cartoon scenes. (Single-frame photography meant that each full turn of the crank exposed one frame, but consistent cranking speed was still important because the duration of the turn controlled the length of exposure, and therefore the brightness of the image.) The Winkler principals had begun to notice that Alice's action in the combination scenes was a bit slow, so the Disneys instructed their cameramen to undercrank these scenes slightly. The unsteadiness of Alice in these shots was a more difficult problem to overcome, and the Disneys attempted to deal with it by using a new, rock-steady tripod.

In October 1924 a new animator, Thurston Harper, was added to the staff. This helped further to relieve the pressure on Walt Disney, who had almost completely withdrawn from animation by this time. One result of his staff's expansion was that Disney, once again, had enough time to use a matte process on the combination scenes in the Alices. From this point on, the illusion of these scenes was complete.

October also brought good news from another quarter: for the first time, an Alice film had been shown in a first-run Broadway theater. The film was *Alice Gets in Dutch,* and it had been shown at the prestigious new Piccadilly Theatre with the Warner Bros. feature *This Woman*, starring Irene Rich and Ricardo Cortez. This must have been doubly gratifying to Disney, for he had lavished an unusual amount of care and expense on the classroom scenes for *Alice Gets in Dutch.* One of the children who had appeared in them was Marjorie Sewell, Lillian Bounds' niece, who turned up in a number of Alices around this time. Within the year she was to become Walt Disney's niece, and years later she retained fond memories of him, not least as a director. "I know one thing," she recalled, "I was absolutely fascinated to see Walt using a megaphone. That excited me, because I thought, oh, that's a real director! Using that megaphone, that was keen."

The news of the Piccadilly booking was conveyed to Disney by the man who had become his principal correspondent in New York, Charles B. Mintz. Mintz had married Margaret Winkler in November 1923, just at the time the Disney studio was first being organized. Although the distribution company retained the name "M. J. Winkler," Mintz came to exercise more and more control over it, especially when his wife became pregnant with their first child.

By the late summer of 1924 Disney found himself corresponding almost exclusively with Mintz, and discovered that Mintz was far more assertive than his wife had been. For openers, Mintz wrote to Disney in August regarding the first two Alices, which had remained something of a sore point with the Winkler organization. Mintz informed Disney that *Alice Hunting in Africa* was actually a liability; the company had *lost* sales by showing it to potential distributors. Now that Disney had, in the distributor's eyes, begun to hit his stride, Mintz wanted him to remake the first two Alices in order to make them acceptable to theaters. Disney, of course, had his hands full as it was, and did not get around to remaking the offending portions of those films until autumn 1924. With *Alice Hunting in Africa*, he lopped off the live-action frame story and put Iwerks to work improving Disney's own animation of the original. Even then the film met with general disfavor, and was written off as a loss. Ultimately the Disneys atoned for it by building a third film, *Alice in the Jungle*, around the live-action footage. (This picture would be released in December 1925, which meant that Virginia Davis appeared in a "new" Alice long after she had actually departed from the series.)

A more serious point of difference between Disney and Mintz involved the content

Virginia Davis McGhee, 1992.

Alice stops a fight between Leon Holmes and Spec O'Donnell in *Alice the Peacemaker.* (Courtesy Virginia Davis McGhee)

Virginia Davis (above) poses for the lobby card (right) in the first series of Alice cartoons. (Courtesy Virginia Davis McGhee)

of the new films. The extensive live-action framing stories of the early Alices had been, as we have mentioned, a necessity; Disney, working alone, could hardly hope to turn out enough animation to fill an entire reel and still meet his release schedule. Now that his animation staff had expanded, such a generous allotment of live action was no longer necessary. It has sometimes been suggested that Disney was taking the easy way out by "padding" the Alices with so much non-animated footage, but the fact is that Disney by now disliked the framing stories and wanted to discontinue them, while Mintz insisted on them. One has to admit that Mintz had a point; the framing stories of the early Alices often have a great deal of charm, and their links with the animated sections are sometimes imaginatively done. But Disney was by this time fully committed to animation, and the last thing he wanted was to become a second-rate Our Gang producer. "After all," he wrote to Mintz in November, "these are cartoon comedies and not kid comedies .... But if we have to put in a live action opening and closing, I am afraid it will just be another one of the ordinary." The shy young Disney of scarcely a year earlier had already been replaced by a professional filmmaker who knew what he was doing and had confidence in his own ideas. In the end, too, his persistence was (in this case) rewarded. Mintz capitulated, and the framing stories began to disappear from the Alices by the end of the year. Disney took special pride in *Alice the Toreador*, much of which centered around an animated audience; in an earlier entry, this would surely have been a gang of live-action children.

But Mintz was as hard-headed as Disney, and as Disney's confidence and determination continued to increase, the clashes between the two men became more frequent and more intense. Soon a mediator became necessary, and officially that role was taken by Nat Levine, the distributor's representative on the West Coast. Mintz first put Disney in touch with Levine in October 1924, and it was the beginning of a loose but long-standing association. Levine was the man who was to establish Mascot Pictures, a low-budget studio specializing in Westerns and serials, within a few years. In the early days of sound, Mascot's talking pictures would be produced with Disney's sound equipment.

Unofficially, Disney's most direct link with the Winkler organization was George Winkler, Margaret's brother. He had a practical working knowledge of filmmaking which Mintz respected, and ultimately he served as a liaison between the Winkler offices in New York and the Disney studio in California. (His intervention helped to persuade Mintz to drop the framing stories.) Disney, too, appears genuinely to have respected Winkler's editorial/supervisory expertise, and the latter not only served as a conciliatory agent, but also contributed one more chapter to Disney's education in the technical side of producing films.

One point that Disney did concede to Mintz involved the number of gags in his films. Mintz felt that the early Alices had been plot-heavy at the expense of laughs, and asked Disney to make his stories less detailed and concentrate on gags. The late-1924 Alices do show a rich proliferation of gags, and this continued to characterize Disney's films well into the early days of Mickey Mouse. Mintz also asked Disney to keep his film titles as "short and snappy" as possible. *Alice Plays the Piper* was, at Mintz's suggestion, changed to *Alice the Piper*.

As the 1924 season drew to a close, it was evident that Disney was maturing as a filmmaker. The 1924 Alices as a group show a blossoming of technique — not only visually, as the animation staff expanded and became more proficient, but also in the development of stories. Disney may personally have found the convention of live-action framing stories an irksome obligation, but, while they lasted, he continued to give them his best. The live-action portions of the 1924 Alices are often quite charming, and Disney seems to delight in exploring the imaginative possibilities of a little girl entering a cartoon world — by contrast with Alice's perfunctory appearances in the essentially all-animated films of later years.

The cartoon gags, too, show a progression, from the simple self-contained gags of the earliest films to more extended and complex scenes, like the suspenseful buildup to

Frame enlargement from *Alice the Piper*. (Courtesy Nederlands Filmmuseum)
Below: Lobby card for *Alice the Piper*. (Courtesy Walt Disney Company)

the dog's charge in *Alice the Peacemaker*. And, as always, Disney's desire to put *more* into his films is evident in the many ingenious throwaway gags: the "Unsafe Safe Co." sign in *Alice's Wild West Show*, or the spear-carrying "caddie" in *Alice Cans the Cannibals*. And the characters on screen have the power to hatch ingenious ideas too; the clever means by which the characters solve their dilemmas in *Alice's Fishy Story* and *Alice the Peacemaker* would soon become a characteristic of Disney films. The Disney brothers may still have been on shaky financial ground, but as their first series ended, it was clear that they were on their way.

The Second Alice Series

Accordingly, the Disney and Winkler forces signed a contract for a second series on 31 December 1924. This time, reflecting the new spirit of confidence that prevailed, the contract called not for twelve films, but for eighteen.

There were, however, some constraints. The principal one had to do with costs; the Disney brothers were enjoined to keep their expenses down. This must have been frustrating to Walt, who was, if anything, anxious to expand. And if he was compelled to make cuts, he was certainly not inclined to make them in the animation department. They must be made somewhere else.

One cut that suggested itself was in the area of live talent. Virginia Davis' contract for the first season had guaranteed her a monthly salary, and her mother was expecting the same provision, or a better one, for the second. Indeed, one of Walt's first letters to her in Kansas City had explicitly proposed a monthly salary of $250 for Virginia's second season. Now the Disneys decided to do away with the contract altogether. Instead they proposed to pay Virginia only for the days when she was actually being photographed — a doubly ominous sign since the live-action footage in the Alices was dwindling. Their idea was that all Virginia's scenes, for the whole of 1925, could be photographed in a total of eighteen days — one day per picture. With eloquent understatement, Virginia recalled: "My mother said, 'Never mind.'"

If Margaret Davis was holding out for better terms, she was unsuccessful; the Disneys merely began looking around for another Alice. This must surely have rankled the Davises, who had moved to California specifically so that Virginia could pursue a career as Disney's Alice. As late as September 1925 Mrs. Davis was writing to Charles Mintz to see whether Virginia might be reinstated. As it happened, she was not, but her career continued to thrive. She went on from the Alice series to play child parts in such features as *The Man from Red Gulch* (1925), with Harry Carey, and the World War drama *A Ship Comes In* (1928). In later years her multiple talents would lead her into a variety of occupations, in and out of show business. In the late Thirties she even went back to the Disney studio, working in the ink and paint department and doing occasional vocal work.

Meanwhile, the Disneys' search for a new Alice brought them a six-year-old actress who was already a veteran. Her name was Dawn Paris, and under the professional pseudonym Dawn O'Day she had been working in motion pictures for years, appearing in films for both Herbert Brenon and William deMille. Her long-term association with Disney might have been an interesting chapter in film history. But if Disney's new financial terms were unacceptable to the Davis family, they were out of the question for Dawn, whose acting income was the sole support of herself and her mother. "Sometimes there was a part," she later recalled, "there was a bit, there was extra work, there was a large part. It went up and down, and there were terrible times where you didn't pay the rent and little things like that." She and her mother were clearly in no position to make themselves dependent on the Alice series, and after a single entry, *Alice's Egg Plant,* they moved on. In time, of course, Dawn's fortunes began to improve. She legally changed her name in 1934 to Anne Shirley, the name by which she is best remembered today.

(One item of interest in the First National sound feature *Three on a Match,* 1932, is

Dawn O'Day in *Alice's Egg Plant.* (Courtesy Carlo Montanaro)

the joint appearance, in the early scenes, of two former Alices. Both Virginia Davis and Dawn O'Day have extensive scenes as the adolescent girls who grow up to be, respectively, Joan Blondell and Ann Dvorak.)

With the departure of Dawn O'Day, the Disneys called back a girl who had already made a trial appearance in *Alice Solves the Puzzle*. (The first film on the 1925 schedule, *Alice Gets Stung*, had been made while Virginia Davis was still at the studio.) The newcomer was a vivacious four-year-old moppet named Margie Gay, and she would become a fixture in the vast majority of the Alice films. Her image represented something of a turning point for the series. Virginia Davis' long curls had been reminiscent of Mary Pickford, and in Dawn O'Day's single appearance she had been cast in the same general mold. Margie, with her stylish bob, rather resembled a tiny Colleen Moore. Marjorie Sewell, who was still making occasional appearances in the live-action scenes, liked her immediately. "I thought she was so cute!"

While these changes were taking place on the live-action front, the animated portions of the films were undergoing an evolution of their own. In particular, the black cat whose early appearances had been so tentative was an established part of the series by the beginning of the 1925 season. He had been christened Julius, and was developing into a full-fledged personality. If he inevitably suggested Felix, he also seems to have anticipated Mickey Mouse; the "clever idea" that saves Alice and Julius from their latest scrape was usually, by this time, Julius' inspiration. With the passage of time, as Disney's interest turned increasingly away from live action and toward animation, Julius would assume more and more of the action. Even before the end of the 1925 series, Alice herself, the nominal focal point of the pictures, would be reduced to brief ritual appearances at the beginning and end of each film, while Julius carried the bulk of the action.

And Julius was not the only animated character to become a "regular" in the Alice series. One of the fascinating discoveries of these years is that the concept of the "gang," which would result in a whole gallery of familiar ongoing characters in Disney's films of the Thirties, actually began much earlier in his work. One example of such a recurring character is the canine cop who first turns up in *Alice the Peacemaker*. That film, with its

Margie Gay, who appeared in thirty-one Alice Comedies in 1925 and 1926. (Courtesy Walt Disney Company)

feud between the mouse and the cat, has strong Krazy Kat overtones, so the dog may initially have been suggested by Offissa Pupp. But he makes sporadic return appearances in other films, continuing for several years.

Another "gang" member who appears in 1925 is the dachshund who can be seen in *Alice Stage Struck*. This dog is never given much of a personality; he exists only for the sake of imaginative cartoon gags built around his ungainly length. Yet he is a durable character for all that. He survives the end of the Alice series in 1927 to turn up in some of the Oswald cartoons, then appears in the first Mickey Mouse, *Plane Crazy* — and continues to crop up in *that* series, serving the same farcical function, as late as 1932.

A more significant debut occurs in *Alice Solves the Puzzle*. The "Bootleg Pete" who appears in this film is none other than the stock villain who will evolve into "Peg Leg Pete" long before the end of the silent period. Watching him develop into that familiar form is one of the pleasures of the Disney silents. For example, he appears in *Alice Solves the Puzzle* as a brute, somewhat similar to his 1930s image — but in subsequent appearances his personality changes subtly. In *Alice Stage Struck,* for example, he emerges as a polished, oily villain, and his personality continues to alter as needed throughout the Alices and Oswalds. Sometimes he and Julius (or Oswald) are merely friendly rivals, at other times they are full-fledged enemies, and sometimes Pete appears as the heroine's father! The wooden leg, too, vanishes and reappears from one film to the next, just as in the later Mickey Mouse films. Pete's appearance at this early date makes him, of all the famous Disney characters of later years, the one with the deepest roots.

By this time Disney was convinced that the only way to surmount the pressures that faced him was to expand his staff. The inking and painting forces were augmented in June 1925 by hiring sisters of the staff members: Ruth Disney and Irene Hamilton. More importantly, at the end of that same month, the expansion of Disney's on-screen "gang" was paralleled by the arrival of the Kansas City "gang:" Rudy Ising, Hugh Harman, and Hugh's brother Walker Harman. Harman, Ising and Max Maxwell (who remained behind in Kansas City at this time) had never abandoned the hope of launching their Arabian Nights studio. They had, in fact, attempted to sell their series to M. J. Winkler in 1924. That attempt had failed, and now Harman and Ising, along with Harman's brother, decided to join the Disney forces in Hollywood while seeking further opportunities there.

This fresh infusion of talent was the push Disney had been waiting for to put his studio on a more solid footing. Ubbe Iwerks was still the "star" of the animation department, but the pressure on him was relieved by the welcome addition of Hugh Harman. Walker Harman pursued his apprenticeship in the business by becoming an inker. Ising, just as in Kansas City, was able to do a little of everything. "I did assistant animation," he recalled, "and some animation, and the camera work. Principally it was the camera and the editing and the printing." His experience in operating an animation camera, along with other phases of production, helped to ease some of the new strain on the payroll. Mike Marcus, who had been the company cameraman for over a year, left the Disney studio — for the time being — within a few days of Ising's arrival. (Another notable departure would take place six months later. Thurston Harper's explosive temper was beginning to make him a liability to the studio, especially now that there were other artists to replace him. He left the Disney studio at the end of 1925, but his animation career continued elsewhere for many years.)

The new studio in which Ising found himself was, as he remembered, not markedly different from the old one. "It was the same group, and almost the same equipment, and the only new people were Ham, his sister, and Roy." The significant change that *was* occurring involved the very nature of animation. The stiff movement of the early films was beginning to give way to a more fluid, flexible kind of movement — first in *objects*, like the safe and fireplug in *Alice Chops the Suey*, and then in the characters themselves. This was because the artists, led by Ubbe Iwerks, were becoming less dependent on the model sheets. "At first, animation was — as I say, you'd trace the character off a model sheet," Ising explained. "But eventually we got out of that habit, and Ubbe was the one that really started that. The model sheets were still made, as sort of a guide. The animators pinned it up on their animation table, but they didn't trace it any more because it limited the animation too much." This allowed the characters to become more plastic and expressive and, in short, to project a more convincing illusion of life. If Iwerks had made no other contribution to the studio, he would deserve to be remembered for this one. It marked the beginning of the smooth, flowing "Disney style" of animation; and one can see it developing, slowly but surely, as the Alice series progresses.

The story content of the films, too, was evolving in interesting ways. Ising confirmed that Disney originated most of the story ideas — but, mindful of Mintz's mandates, was careful to put the stress on gags. "We would sit in the office and they would have a story

From left: Ham Hamilton, Roy Disney, Hugh Harman, Walt Disney, Margie Gay, Rudy Ising, Ubbe Iwerks, Walker Harman. (Courtesy Walt Disney Company)

meeting, Walt and Ham, and Hugh, we'd all sit in on it and work over various gags. Walt would have an idea — well, let's let Alice be a fireman in this one, or let's let Alice go fishing, or whatever it was. And then we'd work up whatever the type of thing was, fire gags or fishing gags. And then Walt would put them all together to tell the story. He'd try to come up with an idea of continuity, he'd sort of work that out, figure out about how long a scene should be, and who was the animator. Or maybe one evening when we met at his house, or our apartment, maybe we'd talk a story gag over too, for the next picture or something."

The stories that emerged from this process were beginning to take on a recognizable Disney quality; indeed, a number of the gag and story ideas which began to appear about this time would be reworked and developed in the later, more famous films. (One obvious example is *Alice Rattled by Rats*, which would be remade in 1929 as *When the Cat's Away*, the sixth Mickey Mouse cartoon.) The occasional references to other contemporary films continued, as in *Alice's Tin Pony*, the title of which suggests John Ford's *The Iron Horse* of the previous year. And from time to time there were, as well, references to other events in contemporary American life. The I.W.W. (Industrial Workers of the World), diminished in importance since the war but still in existence, came in for some mild ribbing in *Alice's Egg Plant*, and the controversial subject of bootlegging turned up in *Alice Solves the Puzzle* — two years before it was given a more serious treatment in MGM's *Twelve Miles Out*.

Inevitably, the content of Disney's films was influenced by other cartoons being made at the same time. Again, the obvious comparison is with the Felix cartoons, although both the design and the personality of Julius are subtly different from those of Felix. Ising remembered that the Disney artists liked the Felix and the Aesop's Fables series, but were less enthusiastic about the Fleischer studio's films. "In fact," he said, "we never did like the New York film ideas. If you look at the films, you'll see that we really developed a whole different type of humor than back there. Back there, some of it was kind of distasteful." This line of demarcation would be more clearly drawn during the Thirties, when Fleischer's dark, gritty, urban cartoons would have practically nothing in common with Disney's sunny, cheerful cartoons. Nevertheless, the Fleischer influence does show in a number of Disney films of the silent period — most apparently in the "inkwell" opening and closing of *Alice Chops the Suey*, but also in the wildly imaginative transformations of objects that were becoming more frequent in 1925.

The Fleischer influence is particularly pronounced in *Alice Chops the Suey*. Opposite: Walt gets married and grows a mustache. Posing with Lillian Bounds Disney in front of the Kingswell storefront studio about 1925. (Courtesy Walt Disney Company)

One trait which Julius definitely shared with Felix the Cat by this time was the creative use of his tail. Disney had begun to use tail gags in his Kansas City films, but during his years in Hollywood they became more profuse and imaginative. A comprehensive catalogue of *all* the uses to which Julius' tail was put would fill a book longer than this one; it becomes a whip in *Alice's Egg Plant*, a unicycle in *Alice Chops the Suey*, a derrick and a ladder in *Alice the Jail Bird*, and so on. This posterior source of gags would be a reliable standby for Disney for a number of years, continuing into the early Mickey Mouse films (*Gallopin' Gaucho*, for example).

Another interesting development during this period is the clever animation of words as they appear on screen. The handicap of having to rely on written words is transformed into an asset when those words come to life and participate in the action — as when, in *Alice Stage Struck*, Julius threatens to make the Bear "eat his words," and then does just that. Such gags would later be abandoned, but during 1925 they flourished briefly.

Ising's memories also shed some valuable light on the materials the studio was using at this time, including the pencils used by the animators. "We used Eagle pencils, they were called; they were brown cedar pencils, and the lead was never exactly straight down the center. I guess they drilled through the piece of cedar and plugged the cylinder with lead, or something. But they were a penny apiece, I think, or a few cents apiece; that's the reason we used them." The leads were prone to frequent breakage, a constant

irritation for the animators. The cels, too, were a far cry from the cels of later years. "We used to wash cels," Ising said. "When the picture was finished we'd wash the cels off and use them again and again and again, until they got too many pen scratches. I think they were made by DuPont, and DuPont actually worked with us on developing them, so the cels got thinner and thinner. But the first ones were, I would say, almost a sixteenth of an inch thick; they were pretty heavy." The biggest problem with the cels' thickness was that their density showed on the screen, especially when a character changed cel levels. If an active character stopped moving, and the cameraman overlaid his cel with those of a new character who had assumed the action, the change would be painfully obvious — as with the two quarreling roosters in *Alice's Egg Plant* who keep changing colors. As the cels were refined this problem became less noticeable, but it would not be entirely eliminated for another seven or eight years.

The new influx of talent brought with it many advantages, but it also meant that the staff had once again outgrown its quarters. Consequently, in the summer of 1925, the Disneys took what would prove to be one of their most momentous steps of the year. On the sixth of July they paid a deposit for a vacant lot at 2719 Hyperion Avenue in Hollywood, and soon construction was in progress for a new studio. Thus was born the fabled Hyperion studio, the scene of so many Disney triumphs. Over the next dozen years, with countless additions and renovations, this studio would see the birth of Oswald the Rabbit, Mickey Mouse and the Silly Symphonies, and the production of *Snow White and the Seven Dwarfs*. In time, *all* of Disney's classic early features would be conceived at the Hyperion studio. It is important to remember that this studio, unlike previous locations, was not a converted office, but was planned and built specifically as an animation studio. Important, too, that this legendary site was brought into being by the Alice Comedies.

By this time, clearly, Disney's attention was focused more than ever on animation, at the expense of live action. The live-action footage in the Alice films was continuing to dwindle. At the beginning of 1925 the Disneys had foreseen photographing all Alice's scenes for the year's eighteen films in eighteen days; by the end of the year, as Rudy Ising remembered it, considerably less time per picture was required. "We'd photograph about three pictures at one time, in one day," he said. "So in other words, if she was a fireman, it would be Alice the fireman and Alice this and Alice that; those would always be shot about three at one time." He also confirmed that by this time George Winkler, in addition to his other contributions, was doing the live-action camera work. Winkler was an experienced cameraman and, among his other activities, somehow found time during 1925 to photograph the Warner Bros. feature *Eve's Lover*. He was also continuing to act as a buffer between Walt Disney and Charles Mintz.

This was fortunate, for relations between the two men were still strained. They were not helped by a new irritant that assailed Mintz at about this time. There exists among the Disney-Winkler correspondence a fascinating "Statement of Facts," unsigned and undated but apparently written by Mintz, or someone under his direction, in mid-1925. It implies that Disney had defrauded the Winkler interests by representing himself personally as the originator of the Alice series in 1923, when in fact he was "employed" by Laugh-O-grams at the time. It also alleges that "while we were distributing pictures bearing the name 'Alice Comedies,' an assignee of Laugh-O-Gram Films Inc., produced several 'Alice Comedies' and was also distributing a number of these pictures, meaning that there were two people distributing pictures bearing the same names, the rights for which were obtained from two separate sources."

In fact the situation was hardly as sinister as the writer of this document imagined. The only Alice Comedy outside the Winkler series was *Alice's Wonderland*, which was still part of the Laugh-O-gram assets. Along the tortuous trail of the Laugh-O-grams bankruptcy proceedings (which would not be finally concluded until January 1927), the rights to the films had been sold to the New York branch of Pictorial Clubs in January 1924. That organization, trying to recoup its investment, was showing the films on a non-theatrical basis, and of course *Alice's Wonderland*, with its family resemblance to the

Disney, Ubbe Iwerks, Hugh Harman, Irene Hamilton, and Rudolph Ising (with lariat) pose for a gag photo on the Hollywood Boulevard lot. (Courtesy Rudy Ising)
Below: Margie Gay, Walt Disney, & Co. on the occasion of moving into the Hyperion studio. (Courtesy Walt Disney Company)

theatrical series, was the most attractive title in the group. But the rights were about to revert to the Laugh-O-grams estate again in August 1925, when Pictorial Clubs fell behind on their payments.

The brooding tension between Disney and Mintz erupted into open hostility in the fall of 1925. Ever since the first Alice Comedy, when Walt Disney was the studio's only artist, he had been dogged by production deadlines that he could not meet. Even when Ubbe Iwerks and other artists were added to the staff, Disney was unable to catch up — especially with the onset of the 1925 contract, which called for delivery of a new picture every three weeks. The problem existed as late as September 1925; when *Alice Chops the Suey* arrived at the Winkler office on the 28th of that month, it was nearly two months late. But with the addition of the new staff members who had started during the summer, Disney finally found himself in a position to produce his films more quickly. *Alice the Jail Bird* followed *Alice Chops the Suey* by exactly two weeks, and Disney let it be known that he had every intention of making up for lost time. He even offered his artists a bonus for every picture completed under schedule.

But if Mintz had been irritated when the pictures were late, he was infuriated when they began arriving early, particularly when Disney made it clear that he expected prompt payment on delivery. "Don't you think it is about time for you to put on your brakes?" an exasperated Mintz wrote to Disney, invoking the three-week interval specified in their contract. Disney argued that the important clause in the contract was the one which called for delivery of all eighteen films by 15 January 1926, and that he was forced to speed up production in order to meet that deadline. He added that his larger staff necessitated a larger payroll, which he could not meet if his advances came at three-week intervals. This argument showed where Disney's priorities lay, but it was hardly calculated to find favor with Mintz.

Into this atmosphere of bickering and cross-purposes came a new element, one which would have a pronounced effect on the next year's contract. Mintz had been finding the independent states' rights market an increasingly tenuous proposition, and during 1925 he had been casting around for a major company to release his films. (These films included, in addition to the Alice Comedies, the Krazy Kat series, which Mintz himself was now producing in New York.) Late in the year he concluded a deal with Joseph Kennedy's company, Film Booking Offices. The FBO deal guaranteed Mintz a new level of money, prestige and visibility, but it also made heavy financial demands on him, and it specified that no films would be released before 1 September 1926. Mintz wrote to Disney, laying his cards on the table and asking whether Disney wanted to be a part of the new arrangement. After painfully protracted negotiations an agreement was reached, and the contracts were finally signed in February 1926. Disney still had a host of problems to deal with, not least among them the long delay before his pictures would be released — but once they *were* released, they would be entering a new and more highly visible arena. All his problems notwithstanding, the future looked brighter than ever.

The Third Alice Series

The new contract between Disney and Winkler acknowledged the growth that had taken place at Disney's studio during 1925; it called for a total of twenty-six Alices — more than twice the number produced during the first season. The first thirteen of these were to be delivered at three-week intervals, the second thirteen at intervals of two weeks. Disney's flat payment per picture was lowered from $1800 to $1500, but thereafter he was to receive a percentage of the profits. And he wrote to George Winkler in January 1926 with a significant request: "I would also like to have embodied in the contract, the understanding which we had verbally ... that all matters regarding making of comedies are to be left to me."

Mintz's main concern at this point was quality; he was highly conscious of the new status the FBO contract represented, and wanted more than ever to put his best foot

A publicity still of Walt Disney directing Margie Gay in 1926. (Courtesy Walt Disney Company)
Below: Two frame enlargements from *Clara Cleans Her Teeth*, featuring Marjorie Sewell in the title role.

forward. "Please use special efforts on your first few subjects," he wrote to Disney, "so that we can really call them knock-outs." When the films did begin to arrive, Mintz offered them to FBO as a group. *Alice Charms the Fish* was the third film produced in the 1926 series, but FBO selected it as their first release in September. Coincidentally, this was also the first film completed at the new Hyperion studio.

The new contract did attempt to ease the financial strain caused by the long gap in release dates. Although FBO was not to begin releasing the Alices until September, Disney was allowed to start delivery on the first of March. This guaranteed him some income with which to meet his growing payroll; and of course it was a good thing for Mintz too, since it allowed him to build up a backlog of films. Because of this arrangement, some of the Alices did not reach the screen for a very long time after their production. *Alice's Monkey Business*, for example, was finished and previewed at the Iris Theater in Los Angeles on 25 March 1926 — but was not released until 20 September, six months later.

This third series of Alices was marked by some new procedures. One of these was the preparation of scripts. The stories for the earlier Alices seem to have been worked out verbally, for the most part — the invention of the storyboard was still several years in the future — but, beginning with the 1926 series, a number of detailed scripts have been preserved. In another departure, all the films in the 1926 series were copyrighted. Only two previous Alice Comedies had been copyrighted; Winkler had registered *Alice Solves the Puzzle* and *Alice Wins the Derby*, seemingly at random, during the 1925 season. (In August 1925 Mintz, not yet having seen *Alice Chops the Suey*, had requested a script for that picture which he might use as a written description for the purposes of the Copyright Office. When he did see the picture, he was so disappointed in it that he cancelled his request, and instead decided to copyright the two earlier films!) All the pictures in the 1926 schedule were methodically registered by R-C Pictures Corp., one of the parent companies of FBO.

The receipt of an advance for each picture, beginning in March, was of some help — but, because much of Disney's income was dependent on projected profits which were still far in the future, the early and middle parts of 1926 were a lean period for the studio. In order to supplement his reduced income, Disney took on various outside jobs, even as production continued on the Alices. One of these special productions led to a little-known and seemingly unlikely alliance, between Walt Disney and Leon Schlesinger. In later years Schlesinger would become the producer of the Warner Bros. cartoons and, therefore, one of Disney's chief rivals in the animation business. But in 1926 he was the proprietor of Pacific Title and Art Studio, a concern which produced special "art titles" on a free-lance basis for studios that wanted to give their films extra production value. To augment his service still further, Schlesinger began to contract with some studios to produce *animated* titles for their films, then subcontracted those jobs to Disney. One of the films to benefit from this arrangement was Nat Levine's first serial, released by Universal as *The Silent Flyer*. More financial aid during this time of trouble came from the still-supportive Dr. McCrum in Kansas City, who obligingly contracted with Disney for a second dental-care film. The result, produced in August, was *Clara Cleans Her Teeth*.

Clara was produced as economically as possible. Marjorie Sewell Davis later insisted that that was the only reason she was cast in the title role: "Specifically, Walt Disney was my uncle, and he didn't have to pay me very much!" The schoolyard scenes were, Mrs. Davis recalled, "filmed at the L. A. Orphanage, with lots of kids." Filming took place in late August 1926, and a newspaper headline in one scene reflects the nationwide concern at that moment over Rudolph Valentino's illness, which would lead to his death on the 23rd.

Like other children who worked with him during the 1920s, Mrs. Davis retained vivid memories of Walt Disney as a director. "He would act things out himself. If he'd tell you to do something, why, he would go through the facial expressions first himself." The highlight of the film is undeniably the dream scene, in which Clara is "haunted" by Ubbe Iwerks' animated dental-care implements. Interacting with these nonexistent characters was of course a challenge for Marjorie. "I had to open my eyes wide and look scared — well, I don't have large eyes. And he kept saying, 'Open your eyes wide!' And I said, 'I've got them open as wide as I can!' He would open *his* eyes wide and stare at me."

The FBO contract did represent a new level of success for the Alices, but early in May an unexpected consequence surfaced. Mintz received a letter from FBO's agent in Paris, asking to have the animated "word" gags eliminated from the films. The agent suggested that the only English words to appear on the screen should be in the form of intertitles which could easily be replaced by translations. "There is nothing that will militate against the success of these Cartoons," wrote the agent, "so much as the inclusion of English words and expressions which cannot be taken out." This had never occurred to the Disney artists, whose films had never before been so highly visible overseas. By this time they were well into production of the 1926 series, but beginning with *Alice's Brown Derby* the dialogue balloons and animated words began to disappear.

Meanwhile, the artists were continuing to develop and refine their technique. The Alices were beginning to have an increasingly polished and elaborate look, thanks in no small part to the artists' use of labor-saving tricks. It has been written that at this time, or shortly afterward, Disney refused to allow his animators to use "cycles" or other shortcuts in his films — a statement which is easily disproved by the films themselves. The Alices and Oswalds are *filled* with such shortcuts, as are the Mickey Mouse and Silly Symphony films that followed. This is not a criticism of the films; on the contrary, one of the delights of these pictures is the artists' growing proficiency in achieving a maximum of effect through an economy of means. One clever device which begins to turn up in the 1926 Alices is the drawing, or animating, of *half* of an elaborate crowd scene — then flopping it over and using it in reverse on the other half of the screen. Again, this device appears in some of Disney's most lavish-looking Silly Symphonies as late as 1932.

The staff of Disney's studio was actually far less stable than it may appear today; in the mid-Twenties, the survival of an animation studio was built on shifting sand. Harman and Ising continued to work for Disney, but were still nursing the ambition of starting their own studio. Taking a short vacation from Disney, they produced a second Arabian Nights cartoon, *Aladdin's Vamp*, which they managed to bring to the attention of Jesse Lasky. Ising wrote letters to "Max" Maxwell in Kansas City, asking him to come out and join them if Lasky accepted the series. This plan, unlike later defections from the Disney ranks, was still open and above-board; Harman and Ising even borrowed money from the studio to underwrite their venture. (Disney may not, however, have been aware of what Ising's letters to Maxwell reveal: that the pair were hoping to lure Ubbe Iwerks away from Disney if their series was a success.) In any case, Lasky ultimately declined, Maxwell stayed in Kansas City, and Harman and Ising stayed with Disney — for the time being.

Ham Hamilton did leave the studio late in 1926, after some personality clashes with Walt Disney. This caused production to fall behind schedule momentarily, especially as Ubbe Iwerks was married on 5 January 1927 and left for a week's honeymoon. But of course the studio had a backlog of films built up by then — and, as it happened, Hamilton soon returned to the fold. In the meantime, Hugh Harman suggested Isadore (Friz) Freleng, another Kansas City artist, as a replacement for Hamilton. Freleng was working at United Film Ad, where he had replaced Harman upon the latter's departure for California. He was duly hired, and arrived at the studio in January. This was his first experience in a professional animation studio, and it marked another alliance that seems surprising today, for Freleng would ultimately become one of the leading directors at the Schlesinger/Warners animation studio.

As a beginner in animation, Freleng was placed under the wing of Ubbe Iwerks — and, like the other animators who had preceded him, he quickly developed a healthy respect for the master. "Ubbe got the toughest stuff to do because he was the most skilled of the bunch," Freleng later recalled. "One of the things I had to animate was a World War I tank, with the treads on the outside, and it was turning and going off in the distance. It had to get smaller as it went. And I was struggling with this thing; I couldn't draw the tank, to start with. And I was sitting next to Ubbe Iwerks, and Ubbe said, "Well,

let me help you with this.' So he took the sheet of paper and he made a few perspective lines and he drew a tank, one view and then the next position and the next position. And it took him five minutes, and he had it all sketched in. He was really an expert at it. And that's how I learned a little bit about animation, from Ubbe Iwerks."

One of Freleng's memories, of his work on *Alice's Picnic*, is especially significant in retrospect. He had been assigned a scene of a mother cat (referred to in the copyright synopsis as "Mrs. Julius") washing her kittens. The point of the scene was a gag in which she dried the kittens by running them through a wringer; the washing action itself was perfunctory. "All the script said was 'A mother cat bathing the kittens,'" says Freleng. "So I did the scene, and I added one little kitten crawling out of the tub, and he's hanging — he was so small he had to hang on the edge of the tub and then drop down. And then the mother grabbed him and put him back into the tub, and a couple of them were trying to escape, and this was just ad-libbed in there. And then Walt called that to everybody's attention. He says, 'I want you to see this scene.' He says, 'That little kitten didn't just jump out of the water, he climbed up and hung there and dropped down like a little kid would do.' He says, 'Friz did it this way and made him act like a little kid. That's what I want to see in the pictures, I want the characters to *be* somebody. I don't want them just to be a drawing.'"

The significance of this incident may not have been apparent at the time, but it seems enormous today. If one had to single out the most important of Disney's many contributions to the art of the animated film, it would be the concept of "personality animation." "The trick in the early days," Freleng explained, "was just to make [the characters] move — make 'em walk, make 'em run, make 'em turn around, make 'em talk to each other, in pantomime, of course. But you didn't distinguish one from another; they all did it the same. But when Walt got into distinguishing one from another by personalities, then it changed the whole thing." Personality animation is generally considered a product of the Thirties; Disney's *Three Little Pigs*, produced in 1933, is often cited as a breakthrough in establishing personalities in a cartoon. But the incident on *Alice's Picnic* is evidence that Disney was contemplating such an idea at least six years earlier.

Late in 1926 the Disney studio became marginally involved in a dispute with the Bray-Hurd Patents company, which owned a group of patents covering every possible aspect of the use of cels in animation. J. R. Bray had been waging a legal war on Paul Terry for nearly five years, attempting to force him to pay a license fee in return for the use of the cel process. When this litigation ended in a standoff in 1926, Terry's brother John formed a group called the Animated Cartoonists' Association to fight the Bray-Hurd interests. All of this was taking place in New York, which was still the center of the animation industry; Disney, in California, was not involved. But his studio had been using cels for some time, and when Terry contacted him and asked him to join the Association, Mintz encouraged him to do so. By the time Disney raised the money, however, Terry's resistance had crumbled. In the end most of the animation studios, including Disney's, gave in and bought Bray-Hurd licenses. (Earl Hurd, another important animation pioneer and one of the patent owners, was later employed at the Disney studio.)

The end of 1926 brought with it a change that has escaped the notice of most writers. It is an established fact that Virginia Davis, Dawn O'Day and Margie Gay all played Alice at various times; what is less well-known is that there was a *fourth* Alice in the series. Her first appearance came in *Alice's Circus Daze*, which was completed and shipped in January 1927. Charles Mintz had not been expecting the change, and immediately wrote to Disney, demanding to know why Margie Gay had been replaced. "I believe it is all a misunderstanding," Disney replied. "In the first place, George and Nat picked her. They made a screen test and George told me to go ahead and use her." He also offered to bring back Margie, but Mintz now remembered that he had indeed authorized the change, and gave it his official blessing.

Who was the new girl, and why was she brought in? Much of this incident is shrouded in mystery. Our first clue to the girl's identity was a letter which Disney

A publicity still of Julius and the gang celebrating Margie Gay's sixth birthday in 1926. (Courtesy Walt Disney Company)

received in 1941, from a lady who claimed to have played Alice in the series, signed "Lois Hardwick." A tell-tale monogram "L" that appeared on the young girl's hat during a test photo session seemed to verify the identification. But only as we went to press did we discover confirming evidence. On 14 April 1928, *Universal Weekly* carried the following item on page 20:

"Little Lois Hardwick, popular child screen star, has been engaged by the Stern Brothers to play the role of Mary Jane in the new Buster Brown Comedies, projected for next season. She has been seen in many pictures, including a number of Alice Comedies, and in such feature productions as *Seventh Heaven*, *The Enemy*, *The Crowd*, *Lilac Time*, and others."

Lois Hardwick, the final Alice, in *Alice the Whaler*.

Other changes were in the air as the year 1927 dawned. For one thing, Mintz's ideas on footage requirements were definitely changing. In 1925 he had very nearly rejected *Alice Chops the Suey* because, at just under 600 feet, he thought it was far too short. ("You can believe me," George Winkler wrote to Disney, "when I say that it was only my intercession that saved you from getting this picture back.") Now, less than eighteen months later, Mintz's position was virtually reversed. His contract with FBO required him to furnish 100 prints of each subject, and any excess footage increased his costs considerably. Now, when *Alice's Circus Daze* reached his office at 648 feet, he complained to Disney that it was too long! Disney offered to guarantee a maximum length of 600 feet for the pictures if Mintz would authorize a minimum of 550 feet. At this Mintz softened his tone, saying he agreed with Disney that 550-600 feet would be an ideal range for the Alices, but that the FBO contract called for 600 feet per picture. (For the following year's contract, a new clause was added which did stipulate a minimum of 550 feet.)

The most important change that the new year brought with it was the imminent demise of the Alice series. Disney was feeling increasingly restricted by the format of the Alices. The combination of little Alice and his animated characters had seemed, in 1923, "something new and clever in animated cartoons!" Now, four dozen films and nearly four years later, it was merely a burdensome obligation. The films had become Alice Comedies in name only; more than ever, the action was carried by Julius the cat instead, while Alice's appearances seemed tacked on as an afterthought. (The title of *Alice Foils the Pirates*, for example, was a real misnomer. Alice was *captured* by the pirates and spent most of her captivity offscreen, and it was Julius, coming to her rescue, who foiled them.) By now it was abundantly clear that Disney's heart was in animation, and he longed to be free of the restrictions of the Alice format. Accordingly, it was agreed that the current Alice series would be the last, and would be followed by an all-animated series.

The new series, however, would not be built around a cat. Disney, as we have mentioned, had never been entirely comfortable with Julius, whose existence certainly seemed to owe something to that of both Felix and Krazy Kat. Now that Disney's films had achieved a certain success of their own, such slavishness was no longer necessary and, indeed, was perhaps undesirable. "I am negotiating with a national organization," Mintz wrote cryptically in January 1927, "and they seem to think that there are too many cats on the market." The national organization was Universal Pictures — another step up in prestige — and they decreed that the new character was to be a rabbit. Disney and Ubbe Iwerks were hard at work on rabbit designs by January, long before the end of production (let alone release) of the Alices.

To Disney's credit, however, Alice's dwindling role in the pictures was the only onscreen evidence of his dissatisfaction with the format. Even as the Alice series came to an end, the final entries showed no flagging of inspiration or effort. The look of the pictures was more lavish than ever, and the gags were increasingly plentiful and imaginative. All in all, Disney could well afford to be proud of the Alice films. During the course of their production he had proven himself as a producer, and had built up an animation studio that was the equal of any in the business. The popularity of the Alices was demonstrated once again in the early days of sound, when the Raytone company

Test shot of Lois Hardwick, the fourth and final Alice, as the young sophisticate. (Courtesy Walt Disney Company)

Lois Hardwick, usually misidentified as Margie Gay, surrounded by Disney and his staff. Back row from left: Walker Harman, Ubbe Iwerks, Hugh Harman, Rudy Ising, Friz Freleng, Roy Disney. (Courtesy Walt Disney Company)

Snapshot of the Disney staff in front of the Disney Brothers studio at Kingswell Avenue in 1925. Photo taken by Walt Disney. From left: Irene Hamilton (inker), Rudy Ising, Dorothy Munson (inker), Ubbe Iwerks, Rollin Hamilton, Thurston Harper, Walker Harman (inker), Hugh Harman, Roy Disney. (Courtesy Walt Disney Company)

Notes

1. This contract date has since been regarded as the official beginning of the Disney studio.

2. Letters from Disney to Margaret Davis. Courtesy of Virginia Davis McGhee.

3. Alva Johnston, *Woman's Home Companion* (July 1934), 93.

4. Diane Disney Miller (as told to Pete Martin), *The Story of Walt Disney,* New York: Holt, 1956, 91.

added music and effects tracks to many of the 1925 titles and reissued them. This may seem a dubious honor, considering the irritating music and sound effects that were inflicted on the pictures, but we can be grateful that it was done. In many cases, the Raytone reissue versions are our only surviving prints of these delightful cartoons.

OSWALD THE LUCKY RABBIT

As the year 1927 dawned, Charles Mintz was in a better bargaining position than ever. His pictures of the previous year, released through FBO, had been successful enough that he could take his cartoon series to the majors. Accordingly he had placed his own Krazy Kat series with Paramount Pictures, and arranged for Walt Disney to release through Universal.

This was a major breakthrough for Disney, assuring him greater distribution, more prestigious bookings, and far more aggressive marketing. In addition, Universal supported his own ideas about replacing Julius with a more original character. There has been some disagreement among modern writers as to who actually originated the rabbit character, but the evidence suggests a collaboration between Disney and the Universal publicity forces. Credit for the character has sometimes been given to Charles Mintz, but in fact he would have been much happier to continue with the status quo. When Disney sent him an assortment of rabbit sketches for approval in January 1927, Mintz simply referred the whole matter to Universal. "If it were up to me," he grumbled, "I would say leave everything stand just as it is."

As Disney and Ubbe Iwerks experimented with the design features of the rabbit, they concentrated on his large feet and, especially, his ears. Iwerks, and hence the studio, was evolving a drawing style built around circles, which had an inherent graphic appeal *and* were easy to animate. The emphasis was on a more flexible kind of movement and a rounded design that virtually eliminated the sharp points of Julius' ears, peg nose, whiskers and teeth. But a rabbit obviously must have long, straight ears, and to animate them effectively required some experimentation. As the experiments continued, the mice in some of the late Alices (*Alice the Whaler* and *Alice in the Big League*, for example) suddenly turned up with long ears!

The rabbit's name was also left up to Universal; the name "Oswald" was reportedly selected by P. D. Cochrane, the head of Universal's publicity department.[1] Disney would later tell his daughter Diane that the name was literally drawn out of a hat. Universal had not released a cartoon series in years, and began to promote Oswald with extensive and enthusiastic ads in the trade press — although, curiously, the rabbit in their earliest ads had not the slightest visual resemblance to the Disney-Iwerks design.

The rabbit's design and name had been established by mid-March, and Disney and company started production of his first film, *Poor Papa*. This picture concerned Oswald's efforts, as an unwilling father, to stop a fleet of storks from delivering ever-greater quantities of baby rabbits to his home. The confrontation quickly escalated into all-out war, Oswald fending off the storks with a shotgun while the babies continued to issue from the chimney, the windows, and the water faucet.

The film was finished by early April 1927, and Disney lost no time in shipping it East to

Poor Papa: original head title.

Mintz and Universal — who promptly rejected it. In an irate telegram to Disney, Mintz complained that the rabbit's first vehicle should have shown him to better advantage: "There are so many other characters that at no time is Oswald outstanding." He thought Oswald sloppy and fat, and advised Disney to make him "young and snappy-looking with a monocle."

Universal's front office was even more pointed. In a list of complaints about the cartoon, they declared: "There is too much repetition of action. Scenes are dragged out to such an extent that the cartoon is materially slowed down." Not only was Oswald unfunny, "the picture is merely a succession of unrelated gags, there being not even a thread of story throughout its length." Disney's reply, quoted in Bob Thomas' biography, accepted the criticism of the rabbit, but rose to defend Ubbe Iwerks, "whom I am willing to put alongside any man in the business today." He agreed, however, to make Oswald a "younger character, peppy, alert, saucy and venturesome, keeping him also neat and trim." (*Poor Papa* was quietly slipped into the release schedule a year later. In 1932 Disney would remake it, with Mickey Mouse, as *Mickey's Nightmare*.)

With Oswald's first film at least temporarily shelved, Disney tried again. *Trolley Troubles* featured Oswald as the conductor of a trolley car which, as Friz Freleng recalled, "looked just like the one Fontaine Fox drew in 'Toonerville Trolley.' That impressed me, because I had been an admirer of Fox's stuff." (This was an interesting coincidence, since Disney's earliest pictures at the Newman Theatre in Kansas City had frequently appeared alongside Fox's live-action Toonerville shorts.) *Trolley Troubles* included a scene in which Oswald, trapped on the runaway car, acknowledged his "lucky" nickname by detaching his own foot and rubbing it on his back. Freleng recalled that he was given this scene to animate. "And I was questioning: 'What do I show when his foot's taken off, do I show a bone in there or what?' And Walt made an issue of it because I didn't know what to do, and of course he never thought of it either, at the time. But when I said, 'What do I do, do I show a bone?,' then everybody started laughing, and nobody knew, really, what to do. Nobody ever thought about that."

This time Disney wrote to reassure Mintz that, whatever the rustic implications of a title associated with the "Toonerville" strip, he was streamlining his rabbit. "We are changing the rabbit still more from the way he looks in this picture. We have eliminated the suspenders and changed his face considerably in the third one."

The second Oswald, unlike the first, was eagerly welcomed by Universal. With all the promotional fervor the studio could muster, *Trolley Troubles* was given an enthusiastic boost in the trade press, and enjoyed the benefit of big openings on both the East and West Coasts. In New York it premiered at the recently-opened "cathedral of the movies" itself, the Roxy, while at the Criterion in Los Angeles it was featured in marquee lights alongside *Flesh and the Devil*. Bookings by the prestigious Balaban and Katz chain quickly followed, as did enthusiastic trade reviews.

Today we tend to think of Oswald the Rabbit as a transitional character bridging the gap between Julius the cat and Mickey Mouse. Freed from even the limited live-action constraints that had bound Julius in the latter stages of the Alice series, Oswald exploded with ebullient energy and high spirits. Judging by contemporary reviews, audiences readily responded to this, as they would to Mickey Mouse within two years. *Motion Picture News* found the fourth Oswald, *Great Guns*, "chock full of humor" and predicted: "This series is bound to be popular in all types of houses if the present standard maintained."[2] By the end of the year, *Moving Picture World* reported that the Oswald series had "accomplished the astounding feat of jumping into the first-run favor overnight."

Great Guns: original head title.

Although the pace, invention, and skillful animation of the Oswald films help to explain their success, it is also true that they followed live-action Hollywood conventions more closely than had the Alices. Unlike Julius, Oswald became a conventional romantic lead. He was, in fact, an incorrigible ladies' rabbit, unable to resist an opportunity for romance — even when he knew in advance that his dalliances would put him in danger, as in *Oh, What a Knight*. Mickey Mouse would inherit this trait for a brief time — most notably for his first appearance in *Plane Crazy*, in which he forced his attentions on

Minnie in an airplane — but would quickly develop a capacity for self-control which Oswald had never learned.

Once the implicit misogyny of *Poor Papa* was past, Oswald, in keeping with his amorous nature, had a girlfriend in the majority of his films. In *The Banker's Daughter* and *Oh, What a Knight* he experimented with cross-species relationships by appearing opposite a female cat, but the girlfriend who appeared on a regular basis was a rabbit like himself, eventually christened Fanny. This precedent, of course, helped to pave the way for the pairing of Mickey and Minnie Mouse, by which time Disney was able to transcend the conventions and create a unique and charming relationship. But for the most part Oswald played the role of either the love-sick swain or the henpecked husband.

Along with Oswald and Fanny, the "gang" of supporting characters continued to appear. The dachshund who could contort his body into any required shape continued to appear in such films as *The Ocean Hop* and *The Banker's Daughter*, and even the Offissa Pupp-like dog made an occasional appearance. Pete, of course, was still on hand. In the late Alices his appearance had evolved in a less menacing and more buffoonish direction, and he continued that trend in the Oswalds. His artificial limb was still optional, but it appeared often enough that he was explicitly dubbed "Peg Leg Pete" in at least two of the Oswalds: *Sagebrush Sadie* and *Ozzie of the Mounted*. (In the latter film he was also known by another favorite alias of this period: Putrid Pete.)

If Disney had been anxious to speed up his productions, he got his wish with the Oswald series. The two-week production schedule, once a voluntary effort on Disney's part, was now required by Universal, for their contract called for twenty-six pictures within a year's time. In order to meet the increased demand, Disney began hiring animators again. Ham Hamilton, whom Friz Freleng had been hired to replace, was back at the studio within a few months, and new faces began to appear on a regular basis. "Max" Maxwell, a veteran of Laugh-O-gram days who had remained behind in Kansas City, finally made the trip to California and joined the Disney forces in 1927.

One particularly notable artist, Les Clark, signed on just as the Oswald series was getting under way. Clark would continue his career at the studio for more than three decades, proving himself a valuable asset to the animation department. Eventually he would become a member of that elite group known as "the Nine Old Men," the first member of that group to join the studio. Another notable name, Johnny Cannon, appeared on the studio roster in July 1927. Cannon would make his mark as one of the leading Mickey Mouse animators in the 1930s. In the beginning, of course, these and other artists functioned as assistants to Ubbe Iwerks and Hugh Harman, Disney's two front-rank animators.

Even as some employees were arriving, of course, others were leaving. One departure of note was that of Rudy Ising, who left in March 1927. Ising had performed a variety of functions at the studio for nearly two years, but principally served as the animation cameraman — a job that aggravated his habit of falling asleep. "Camera work was pretty monotonous once you started to photograph," he explained, "and I used to fall asleep between frames. And then we had a motor drive — you'd pull the cord and it would click, and the motor was kind of noisy, and every once in a while I'd fall asleep." This could be an expensive habit, for a single mistake could ruin many hours' work and require costly retakes. Some camera accidents had been allowed to remain in the Alices (in *Alice's Orphan*, for example, some silverware repeatedly vanishes from a table and then reappears on it), but with his new release schedule, Disney could not afford to take chances. Ising, for his part, had other interests besides animation; he was particularly interested in portrait photography and wanted to pursue it. "So actually I said, 'Look, Walt, why don't I just leave, and you can get somebody else for your camera.' And he said, 'No, I don't want to do that,' and I said, 'Yeah, but I'd just as soon, why don't I leave.' And that was it." Mike Marcus, who had photographed the animation before Ising arrived, was back at the same job within a week of Ising's departure.

In addition to the hiring of new artists, other measures became necessary to cope with the increased production demands of the Oswald series. For one thing, the handful

Original frame from Oswald tail title, "The End."
Opposite: "Diabolically yours, Putrid Pete" – the 1927 version of Mickey's nemesis, Pegleg Pete. (Courtesy Walt Disney Company)

Diabolically yours
Putrid Pete

The chorus of rascally long-eared mice are even more prevalent in Oswald posters than in Oswald cartoons. On this and the following pages, four sketches for Oswald posters: *Harem Scarem*, *The Mechanical Cow*, *Sky Scrappers*, and *The Ocean Hop*. (Courtesy Walt Disney Company)

10. L. S. exterior town---snow covered buildings---corner of
building in center scene---Pete runs on from right---Oswlad
rides on from left---they meet in center scene and collide---
knock both unconscious---Oswald's horse is thrown from scene--
Pete looses his snow shoes and sits on ground at left side of
scene in a daze---Oswald on ground at right side with head
knocked down into collar of miss fit unsriform.

11. Semi C. U. Oswald laying on ground with head missing---he
sticks his head out collar in dazed condition---he recognizes
Pete off scene and crawls out collar and leaves coat laying
on ground as he runs off toward Pete.

12. Semi L. S. Pete sitting on ground in dazed condition---Oswald
runs in---recognizes him as the man he wants---taking
advantage of Pete's dazed condition, he acts very brave and
pulls very large pistol out of holster---points it at Pete
and tells him he is under arrest. Pete comes to---sees
Oswald with big gun---gets sore and gets up ready to grab
Oswald---all the time, Oswald is trying to make Pete throw
up his hands---when Pete ignores his command and continues
getting ready to grab him---Oswald becomes scared, aims gun
and pulls trigger---hammer on gun flops down---ball can be
seen going down barrel---oozes out end into large ball---
hits Pete in stomach, dents it in and bulges out back---
springs back---hits Oswald and knocks him down---Pete jumps
on him---picks him up and starts choaking---each time Pete
choaks, Oswald's tongue sticks out longer. When Oswald's
tongue is hanging way out---Pete realizes what he has done--
becomes scared---drops Oswald---glances around quickly and
runs off scene.

13. Semi L. S. dog sled with two large hound dogs and little
Black Scotch Terrior in center, hitched to sled by ropes---
they are sitting down asleep. Pete runs in---hops on sled
and cracks whip---big dogs wake up and start to run, as ropes
draw tight, it flops little dog in air and leaves him
suspended there as big dogs run (move pan)-little dog runs
in air without his feet touching ground---as big dogs run,
their bodies wrinkle up accordian style instead of arching---
Pete glances back in direction of Oswald.

14. Semi C. U. Oswald on ground in dazed condition with about a yard
of tongue hanging out---he gets up wabbly---sees his tongue
hanging out and by pulling tail out on string, he pulls
tongue back in place---lets go tail and it springs back to
shape---he sees Pete running away and starts pursuit.

Page from scenario for *Ozzie of the Mounted*. Opposite: Page three (panels 9-14) of story sketches for *Ozzie of the Mounted*. (Courtesy Walt Disney Company)

The changing shape of Oswald. Responding to complaints from Universal, Disney modified Oswald's original country-boy look in *Poor Papa* and *Trolley Troubles*. Universal argued that Oswald should be well-groomed (as their memo noted, "With the exception of Chaplin, important movie comedians are neat and dapper chaps"). Disney obliged them in this early sketch with an Oswald in spats and a cane. Opposite: "Slush and best wishes — Foolish Fanny" Oswald's erstwhile girlfriend. (Courtesy Walt Disney Company)

Much and Best Wishes
Foolish Fanny

of inkers and painters who had sufficed for the Alice series were no longer enough. Hazel Sewell, Lillian Disney's sister, was hired to establish and supervise an expanded ink and paint department. For a time, beginning in the summer of 1927, Disney tried dividing his animation staff into two separate units, so that two pictures could be produced simultaneously. One of the units was headed by Ubbe Iwerks and Friz Freleng, the other by Hugh Harman and Ham Hamilton.

The Universal release of his films represented a new level of success for Disney, and brought with it a number of precedents. One of these was a regular showcase for his films at the Colony Theater in New York. This moderately prestigious theater, opened for films only a few years earlier, had recently been leased by Universal. Disney's Oswald cartoons began to appear on the Colony's screen as early as September 1927, paving the way for the famous opening of *Steamboat Willie* there in November 1928. And the connection did not end there; the same theater, renamed the Broadway, would be the scene of the New York opening of *Fantasia* in 1940.

The Oswald series established another important precedent: it introduced Disney to character merchandising. The Disney-Winkler correspondence indicates that some forms of merchandising had been contemplated during the run of the Alice series; picture books and promotional postcards had both been considered at various times, but neither of these ideas was actually realized. Universal, on the other hand, had a standing policy of exploiting its stars and films through merchandise licensing, and did not hesitate to promote Oswald in the same way. Early in the summer of 1927, before any of the cartoons had been released, an Oswald chocolate candy bar appeared on the market. This was followed in July by novelty buttons bearing the rabbit's likeness, and the spring of 1928 brought the most elaborate promotional item of all: an Oswald stencil set for children. The concept of character merchandising was to have a considerable impact on Disney, whose studio would be kept afloat in the 1930s largely by royalties from the sale of Mickey Mouse merchandise.

It was at this time, too, that Disney introduced a long-standing practice of his own: the giving of bonuses for story and gag ideas that were used in the pictures. This practice, which would enrich the content of his 1930s cartoons *and* steer a number of erstwhile animators to careers in the story department, was established by mid-1927. When Ubbe Iwerks and Friz Freleng set about animating *The Banker's Daughter*, for example, they were working on a story they themselves had conceived. (Freleng also recalled that the pressure of Disney's release schedule was so great that he gave bonuses for every picture completed on schedule!)

The stories for the Oswald cartoons were laid out in the form of small drawings. These were not simply rough sketches, but detailed representations of the intended scenes, sometimes indicating footage. This emphasis on preplanning the visuals was becoming an important element of the studio's method. The Oswald story drawings differed from Disney's later methods in only one important respect: they were made in inflexible groups of six to a page. The concept of the storyboard, on which each sketch was a separate and interchangeable unit, had not yet evolved.

In addition to the drawings, a script was still prepared for each film, and these were becoming more and more elaborate. The earliest Alice scripts had crowded descriptions of ten or twelve scenes into a single page, eschewing delineation of details. A typical scene description from the script of *Alice's Monkey Business*, written early in 1926, reads in its entirety: "9. Flash close-up — Lion doing dance. Shimmies etc., mane comes down and forms skirt. Does crazy stuff. Tiger girl chorus dances in behind lion."

But as Disney became more concerned with the refinement of detail in his films, the scene descriptions became lengthier. By February 1928 he was taking a whole page to describe the opening scene in *Sky Scrappers*. This is the shot description we quoted earlier when commenting on Disney's growing predilection for macabre mechanical animals. But it is worth quoting again to notice how meticulous Disney was becoming over details. "When dirt lands in truck, it smashes body down and flattens rear wheels — raises front end of truck up off ground (not too much) .... NOTE: first time truck goes off

Oswald in Germany. Buster Brown was another Universal comedy series: the girl in the picture is Lois Hardwick, the same actress that Disney used in his 1927 Alice Comedies. (Courtesy Walt Disney Company)

better not start shovel working until truck is almost off so as not to detract." (These scripts also confirm the link between the Oswald and Mickey stories; the *Sky Scrappers* script is a virtual blueprint for the 1933 Mickey Mouse short *Building a Building*.)

It was in February 1928 that Walt Disney made his fateful trip to New York. Production of the contracted Oswald cartoons was nearly complete (though fewer than half of them had been released), and Disney thought he was simply going to negotiate a new contract with Mintz. The Oswald series was clearly a success, and Disney was hoping to raise the price per film from $2250 to $2500.

He was in for a rude awakening. Instead of offering Disney more money, Mintz offered him less. The true situation has since been widely documented: Mintz, with George Winkler's help, had secretly approached Disney's key artists and signed most of them to contracts of his own. He was acting within his legal rights; in the animation business of the 1920s, control over a series and a character rested not with the producer but with the distributor. Ubbe Iwerks had resisted Mintz's advances, but Hugh Harman, Ham Hamilton, and others on the animation staff had felt no particular loyalty to Disney and had readily gone along.

The motive behind Mintz's actions appears simply to have been a greater degree of control over the Oswald cartoons. It was not his intention to crowd Disney out of the arrangement; he took the opportunity of Disney's visit to offer *him* a contract, as he had the others. By this arrangement, Disney and his staff would all have been Mintz's employees, so that both series of cartoons — Krazy Kat and Oswald the Rabbit — would have been under Mintz's direct control. It must have seemed that Disney, with so many of his key artists signed up, would have no choice but to submit.

Charles Mintz was not the first man to underestimate Disney, and he would not be the last. Disney was outraged at what he considered an act of flagrant betrayal, and would have no part of Mintz's proposal. Without hesitation he abandoned his connections with Mintz, Universal, and Oswald the Rabbit. He would finish the films which were required by the current contract, and from then on would pursue his own independent course.

Disney was of course fortified by the knowledge that his star animator, Ubbe Iwerks, was still with him. Even before returning from New York, he instructed Roy to lose no time in signing Iwerks to a new contract. Knowing that he must replace the defecting animators, Disney also began quietly casting around for new artists. His loss of his artists to Mintz at this time is common knowledge; what is less well known is that Disney considered turning the tables. One of the artists he contacted in New York was Bill Nolan, who was currently animating Krazy Kat for Mintz. Nolan was, essentially, the Ubbe Iwerks of the Mintz studio; to have both Iwerks and Nolan under contract would have given Disney an unbeatable animation staff, not to mention poetic revenge on Mintz. In the end, however, Nolan decided to remain where he was.

Mintz was doubly fortunate not to lose his top animator, for he had enough troubles as it was. The Oswald cartoons had been so well received that Universal eagerly contracted for a second series, and Mintz, having lost Disney's services, was obligated to produce them himself — simultaneously continuing production of his Krazy Kat series in New York. George Winkler was quickly deputized to take over the Oswald pictures in Hollywood. In the ensuing scramble to provide sufficient product for the Universal release schedule, the previously rejected *Poor Papa* was dusted off and released, while two other Disney pictures, *The Fox Chase* and *Sagebrush Sadie*, were reissued. When the Winkler-produced Oswalds began to appear, they were cannily interspersed with the last of the Disney entries. (Whether through accidental haste or design, the earliest Winkler Oswalds retained the original title card, with Disney's name in the credits.)

And so, for the time being, Oswald the Rabbit's screen life continued. In the spring of 1929 the rights to the series changed hands once again, this time being produced by Walter Lantz directly for Universal. Lantz continued to produce the Oswalds, without any great distinction, until 1938, when the rabbit quietly faded away. But if Oswald's short life with Disney had accomplished nothing else, it would still be notable for having helped to launch the greatest cartoon character of them all.

Notes

1. This claim was made by Arthur Mann in "Mickey Mouse's Financial Career," *Harper's Monthly Magazine*, May 1934, 715. This article, as its title suggests, dealt with Disney's business history, and it appears to have been based partly on interviews with Disney.

2. Review, *Motion Picture News*, 19 August 1927, 526.

2.   L.S. of Jungle. Two little characters in F.G. skipping rope
     with lion's tail. Monkey using snake as swing. Several
     characters, small, being tossed up onto giraff's head by
     aligator. They slide down giraff's neck and back into water.
     Big hippo asleep in water. Other animals asleep on scene.

Three tantalizing fragments from a lost Oswald, *Africa Before Dark*. The jungle scene survives in three different formats, providing an idea of Disney's early animation procedures.

Above and top: In the script, the jungle scene is described in shot #2. In the story sketches, the jungle scene is roughed out in the second panel. (Courtesy Walt Disney Company)

Left: The background for the same scene. The missing animals, described in the script, were drawn on separate animation cels. This is the only piece of final animation art known to survive from the silent Disney period. (Courtesy S/R Laboratories Animated Art Conservation Center, Westlake Village, CA)

Overleaf: Page from the script for *Africa Before Dark*. Pages 103 to 106: The story sketches for *Africa Before Dark*. (Courtesy Walt Disney Company)

"AFRICA AFTER DARK."

1. Iris opens part way revealing O. wearing hunting helmet and
   holding big gun riding along on elephant's back. As
   elephant walks, Oswald's head remains stationary while body
   and helmet move with action of elephant. Iris opens clear
   revealing elephant riding bicycle instead of walking.
   (Use card board iris.) As rocks come on scene elephant dodges
   them in graceful manner. He feels proud of his accomplishment
   and looks up to O. with a proud smile. As he does, a very
   large rock comes on, he hits it and spills in the dust. Dust
   completely covers characters and as it fades off scene, it
   reveals elephant running on tusks and trunk, and O. hanging
   over side by elephant's tail. O. pulls himself up onto
   elephant's fanny, he is puzzled and sore. He holds onto tail
   and leans over side to tell elephant to stop. As elephant
   skids on tusks and stops, it spills O. off and he lands flat
   on stomach. The elephant unknowingly sits on him. Oswald's
   head is sticking out from under him. When O. yells, elephant
   discovers he is sitting on him and gets up. (Elephant gets
   up like a little kid. Fanny faces camera in an awkward way.)
   Elephant acts sorry. Oswald's body is smashed flat, head is
   normal. O. gets up, looks at body as he turns it at xxxxxxxx
   different angles. O. is sore, he bawls elephant out.
   Elephant gets idea, puts trunk over Oswald's face and by
   pumping his tail he fills O's. body out. O. floats up in air
   and body gets larger than normal. When elephant pulls trunk
   off, air comes out of O. and he flops to ground in sitting
   position. His body is normal. He curses elephant. Elephant
   acts sorry.

2. L.S. of Jungle. Two little characters in F.G. skipping rope
   with lion's tail. Monkey using snake as swing. Several
   characters, small, being tossed up onto giraff's head by
   aligator. They slide down giraff's neck and back into water.
   Big hippo asleep in water. Other animals asleep on scene.

3. Semi C.U. two monkeys playing game of criss cross on tiger's
   back. They scratch selves as they play. Tiger watches game
   with amused smile. The monkey that wins is very tickled.
   The one that looses is sore and argues. As he argues he begins
   to scratch under arm.

4. C.U. of monkey that lost. As he scratches under arm, the flea
   hops in air and lands in center of monkey's back. Monkey tries
   to scratch it but can't reach spot. He goes thru different
   contortions trying to reach spot, but doesn't have any success.
   He gets idea. Takes teeth out, holds them with tip of tail,
   then bites up and down back. Satisfied smile on monkey's face.
   (Note - When he takes teeth out, it leaves his jaws sunken.)
   He catches flea, holds him with fingers as he puts teeth back
   in. Flea gets away. Monkey slaps him with foot and beats him
   unconscious with fist. He pulls out plate, knife, fork and

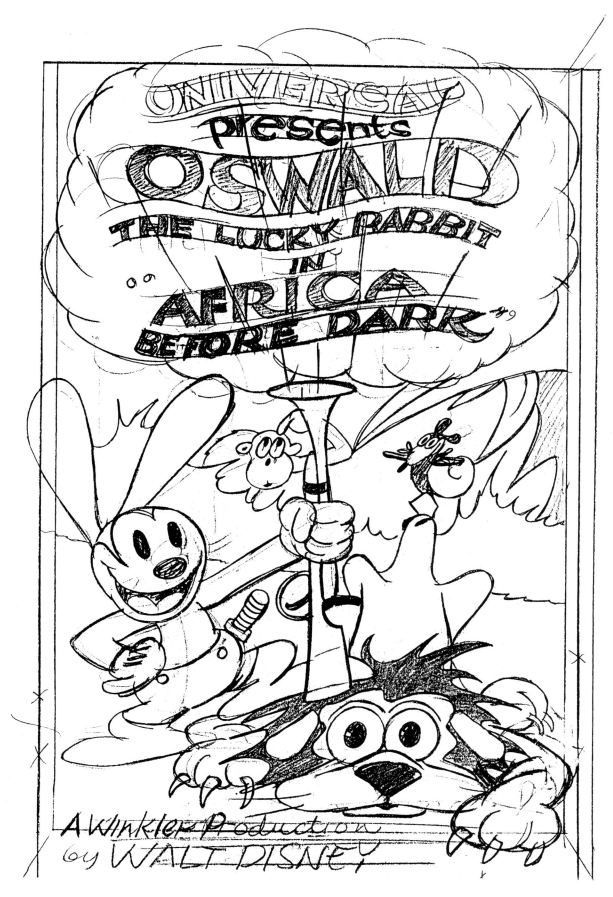

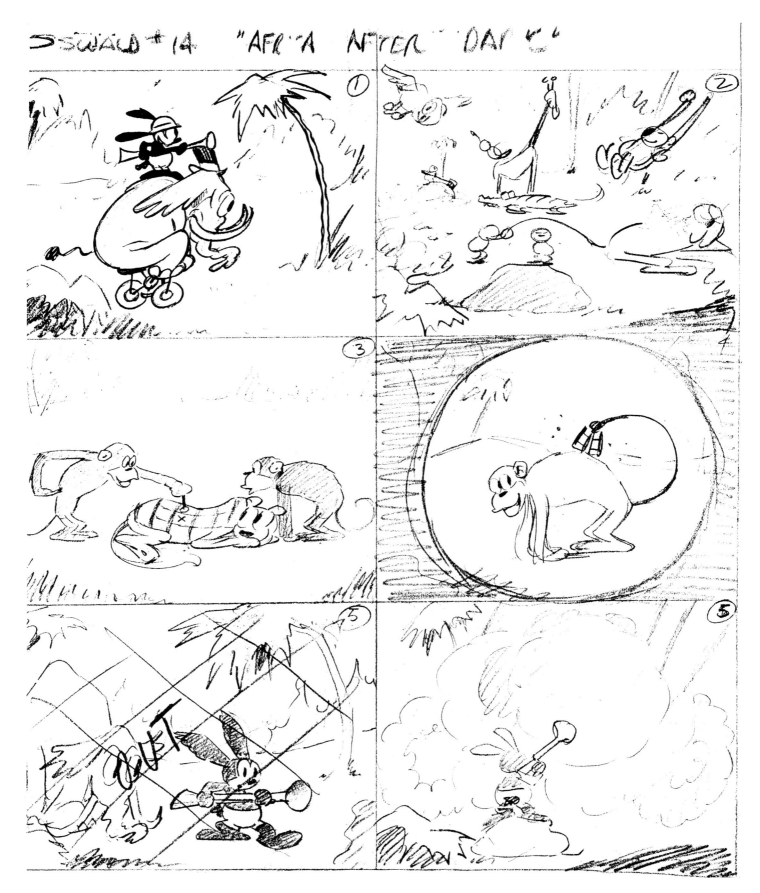

Ride 'em Plow-boy!: the story sketches. Panels 5-13: a remake of the egg-laying production line scene in *Alice's Egg Plant*. Panels 16-24: Disney's first cyclone, a forerunner to the surreal tornadoes that send animals aloft in the 1931 version of *The Ugly Duckling* and *The Band Concert*. Here Oswald turns his milk cow into an airplane. (Courtesy Walt Disney Company)

TITLE - CYCLON

109

24/⊗

50

111

The Vogan Candy Company's trucks in Portland, Ore., all wore Oswald banners for a while, advertising the new chocolate bar named for Universal's cartoon comedy character which has become the candy company's biggest seller.

Universal's Oswald Cartoon Comedies
Backed by Chocolate Bar Tie-Up

THAT short subjects should be backed by the same exploitation ability that helps to make feature pictures well known to the movie going public is one of the cardinal

A 2-column newspaper ad.

principles of the Universal organization. Their "Collegians" series, "Newlyweds," "Buster Browns," "Gumps" International Newsreel, etc., have been tied up with national advertisers, provided with feature accessories and started off in hundreds of houses with campaigns laid out by the Universal exploiteers.

And now come the Oswald comedies, the cartoon series of one-reelers being released by Universal on the 1927-28 program. F. F. Vincent, the Universal exploitation man in the Pacific Northwest, has tied them up in such a way that they have been sold to practically everyone in his territory before they ever reached the

screen, and their fame is rapidly travelling eastward.

The Vogan Candy Company of Portland, Ore., being a live concern and always looking for new ideas, snapped up Vincent's suggestion that they put an "Oswald" candy bar on the market. A very tasty confection was originated which bears the subtitle, "Milk Chocolate Frappe Bar," and an extensive advertising campaign was laid out which includes newspaper space, counter cards, window stickers and banners on all the company's trucks. The bar immediately "took" and is proving the biggest seller the company has ever had. Already shipments have been made to Honolulu and Alaska.

Advertising and the wrapper on the candy bear a cartoon of the "Lucky Rabbit" as he appears in the comedies and his face as well as his name is fast becoming familiar to fans. Wherever these bars are sold they form an ideal exhibitor-merchant tie-up which will benefit the theatre and the man selling the candy equally.

When Vincent promoted the Reginald Denny Fast and Furious Races in Portland, Ore., at a local track in connection with the showing of the picture at the Columbia Theatre, he arranged that "Oswald" bars should be the only confection sold at the track. This helped not only the candy company but Universal, through the wide publicity given the Oswald comedies, and such cooperation might be given in other communities where the bar is sold. Consult your candy dealers.

A window sticker.

The 3-panel counter card used by Oswald dealers.

Posters for *Alice's Day at Sea*, *Alice Hunting in Africa*, and *Alice in the Jungle*. (Courtesy Walt Disney Company)

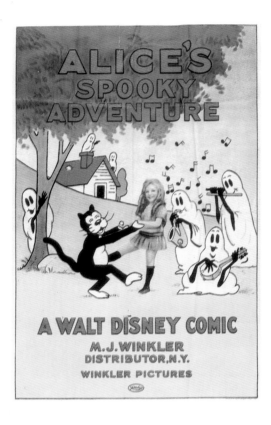

Poster for *Alice's Fishy Story*.
Poster for *Alice's Spooky Adventure*. Music was important even in poster advertising. Little Virginia in a 1920s shimmy outfit dances with her as yet unnamed cat.
(Courtesy Walt Disney Company)

Posters for *Alice the Peacemaker* and *Alice Gets in Dutch*.
(Courtesy Walt Disney Company)

Poster for *Alice Helps the Romance*.

Poster for *Alice the Golf Bug*. Margie Gay poses in her trademark playsuit with the members of Disney's repertoire company. The poster gives Pete ten fingers, as was the Disney custom throughout the silent period. Only in the 1930s did Disney's animators think to streamline hands by giving characters four-fingered gloves. The influence of George Herriman's Krazy Kat can be seen in the abstract, lunar landscape. (Courtesy Walt Disney Company)

Poster for *The Ole' Swimmin' Ole*.

A trade advertisement from *Universal Weekly*. (Courtesy Walt Disney Company)

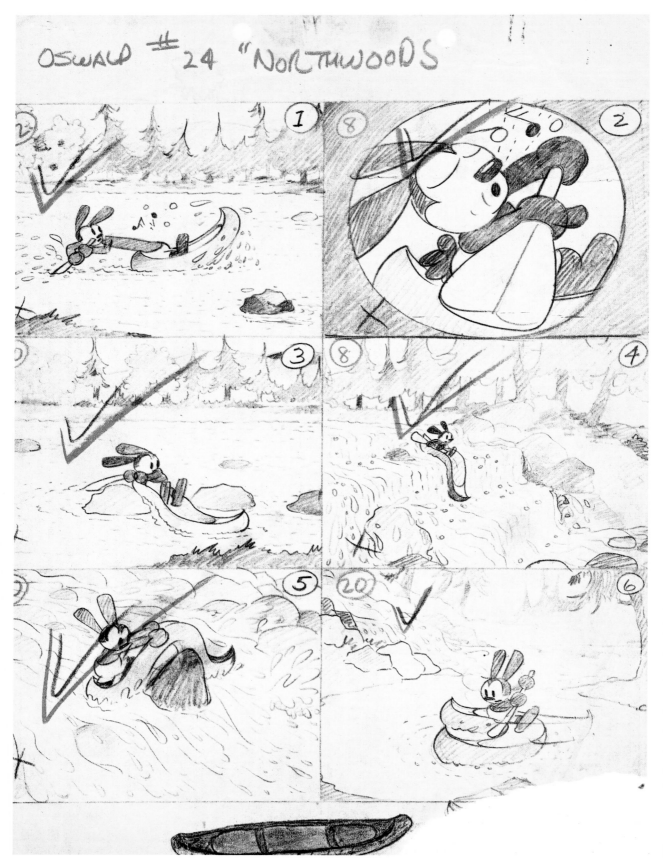

The story continuity sketches for an Oswald originally called "Northwoods" and released as *Tall Timber* illustrate how cartoon stories were worked out in the late 1920s, before the advent of storyboards. (Courtesy Walt Disney Company)

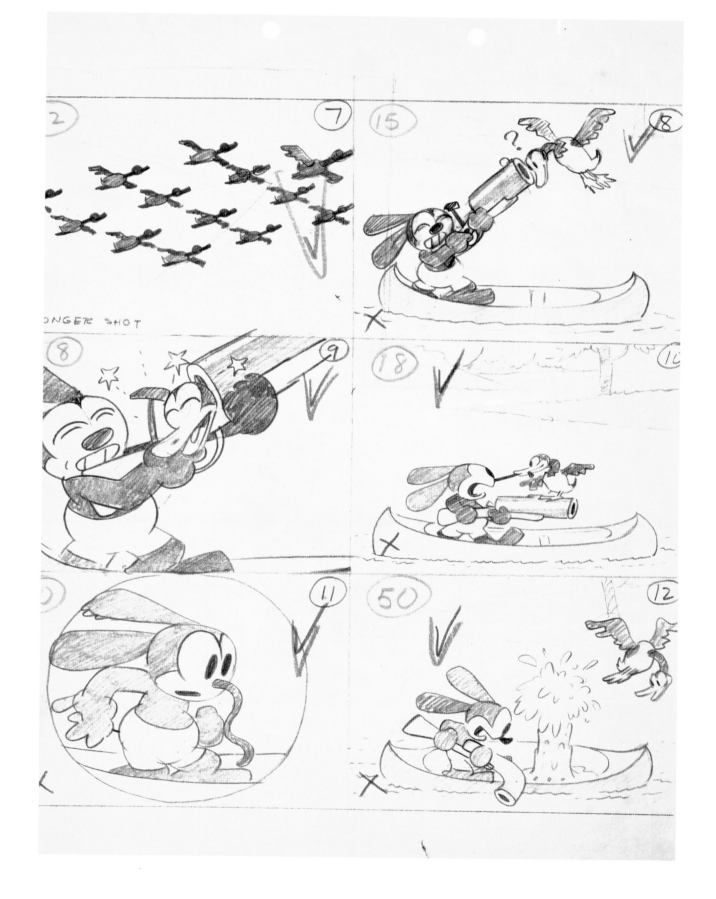

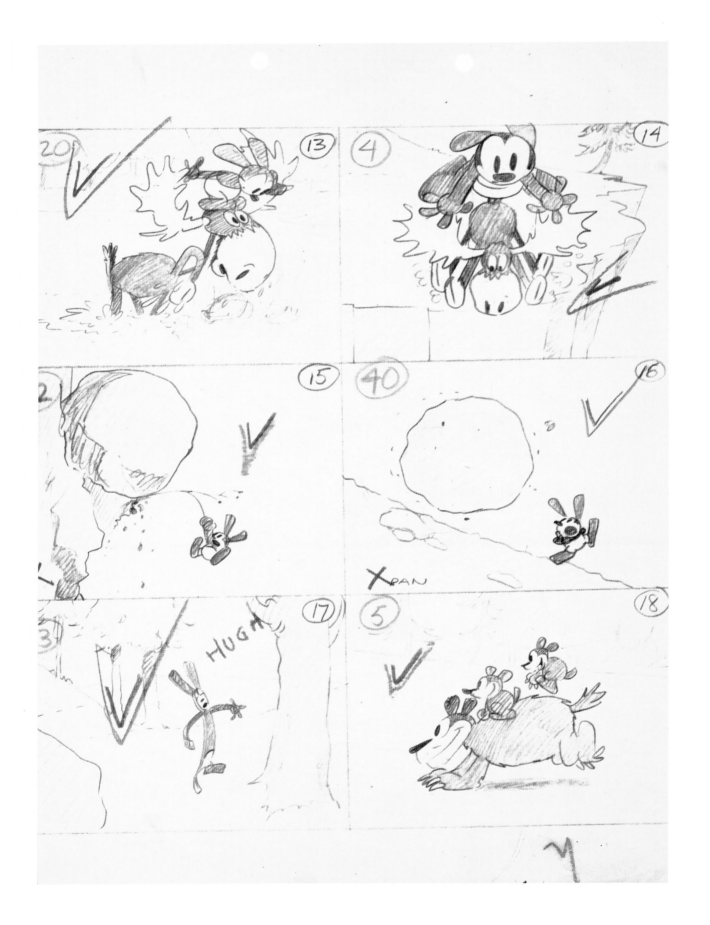

500 FT TOTAL

"Funniest Reel on Market"

—*Miner's Theatre, Collinsville, Ill.*

"Wish we played them every week instead of every two weeks."

—*New Franklin Theatre, New Franklin, Mo.*

"A cheer always goes up from audience when Oswald is flashed across the screen."

—*Majestic Theatre, Memphis, Mo.*

"Oswald comedies making biggest hit of any comedies I have ever run."

—*Lion Theatre, Hammond, Ill.*

"Best I have ever run."

—*American Theatre, Johnston, Ill.*

"Oswald a real hit."

—*Drake Theatre, Drake, Ill.*

Oswald is the creation of Walt Disney. Produced by Winkler Productions. Released by **UNIVERSAL**

OSWALD
THE LUCKY RABBIT

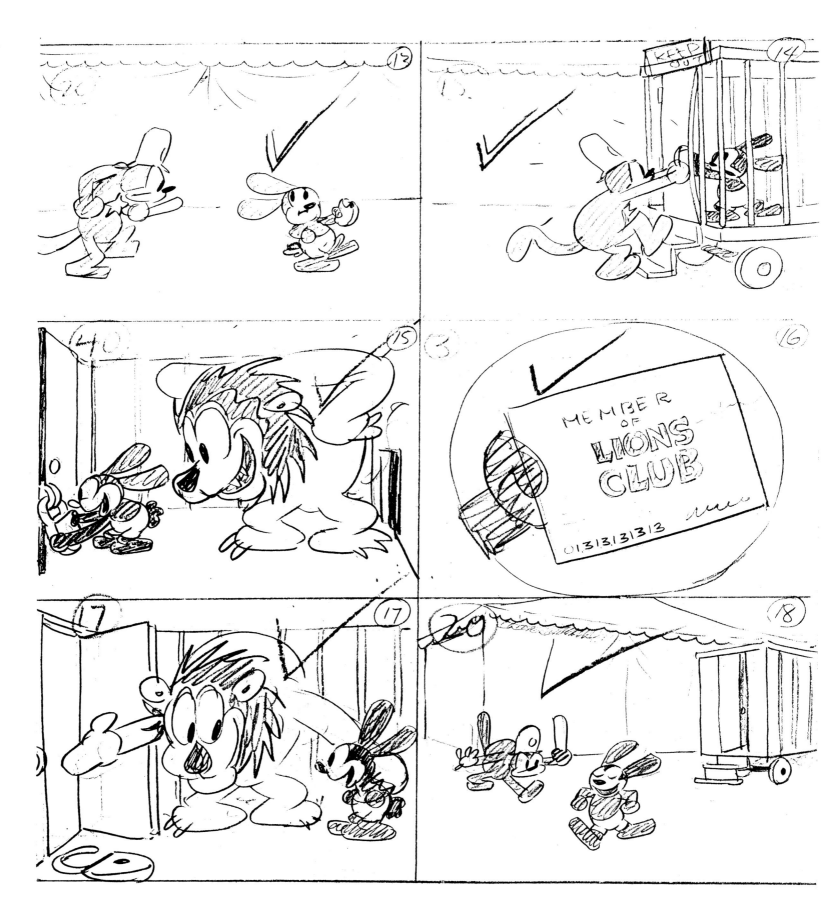

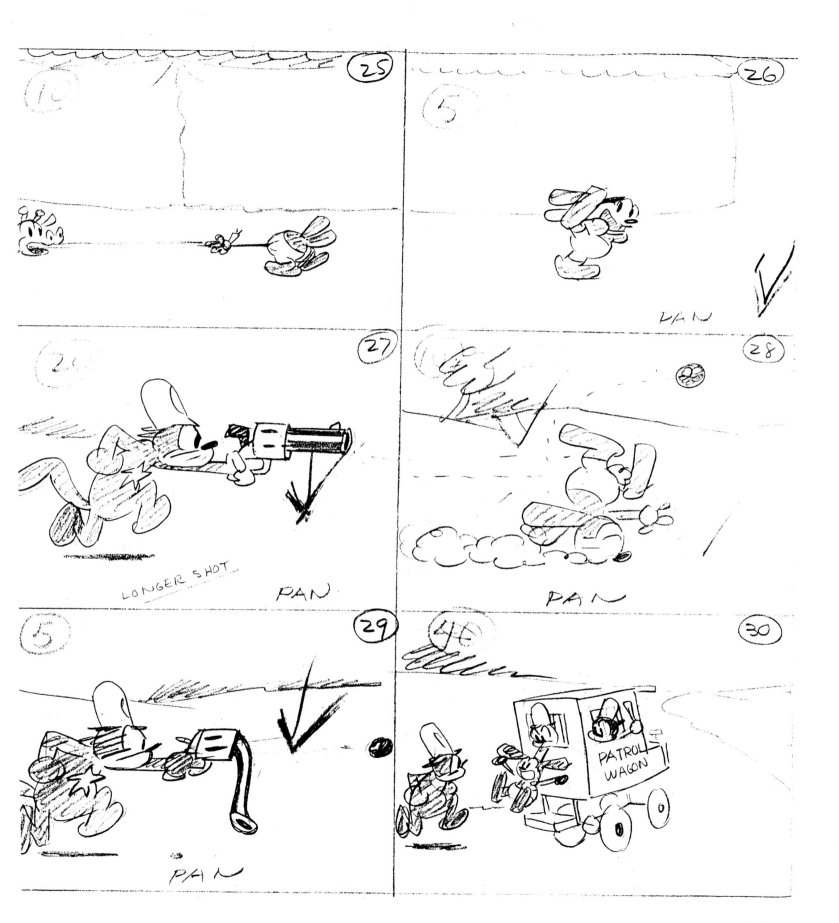

The genetic engineering of Oswald. When Mickey Mouse eclipsed Oswald, the rabbit Mintz had taken away from Disney was streamlined to look as much as possible like the new Disney mouse. This post-Disney Oswald, usually mislabelled Disney's work, is a Walter Lantz design from an early 1930s model sheet. (Courtesy Walt Disney Company; Mickey Mouse copyright Walt Disney Company)

When Walt Disney made a decision, he acted quickly and decisively. Galvanized by the sudden loss of Oswald the Rabbit, he wasted no time on recriminations or reflection, but went to work immediately on a new course of action. The birth of Mickey Mouse in his mind, as he and Lillian made their way back to California by train, is an event shrouded in legend. The story of his naming the mouse "Mortimer," while Lillian opted for the shorter and snappier "Mickey," has been retold innumerable times. We know for certain that Disney arrived back in Hollywood on 18 March 1928, ready to start developing the new character with Ubbe Iwerks. Just over a month later, the Mouse's first film was in production. This was *Plane Crazy*, inspired by Charles Lindbergh's trans-Atlantic flight — a feat which had also provided the basis for the previous year's Oswald cartoon, *The Ocean Hop*.

Disney had learned many important lessons about the film business during his years with Winkler and Mintz, and he had grown tougher. Previously he had simply followed standard procedure in his business dealings; the producer served as a subordinate of the distributor, who controlled all rights to the character and the films. Now Disney resolved never to make himself so vulnerable again. The new character and all his films would be wholly owned by Walt Disney. The "Mickey Mouse" trademark was registered in his name on 21 May 1928, and he copyrighted *Plane Crazy* a few days later.

Plane Crazy.
(Copyright Walt Disney Company)

So anxious was Disney to begin his new enterprise that production of *Plane Crazy* began even as the last of the Oswald films were being completed. Disney assigned Oswald animation to the artists who had accepted contracts with Mintz, while Iwerks, sequestered in a separate office, worked in secret on *Plane Crazy*. This first Mickey cartoon must stand as one of the highlights in Iwerks' career; it was animated in its entirety by one man, in a period of about two weeks. Even allowing for the paucity of crowd scenes and the liberal use of cycles and repeats, this represents a prodigious achievement. Iwerks' daily output on the film was estimated at 700 drawings.

The drawings were finished early in May, while the last Oswald films were still in production, and so the atmosphere of secrecy continued. Just as he had done for the Newman Laugh-O-grams seven years earlier, Disney set up a makeshift studio in his garage. There Hazel Sewell, Lillian Disney, and Roy's wife Edna inked and painted the cels. Then the cels were taken back to the studio at night, and Mike Marcus, the studio cameraman, worked late hours to shoot them after the Oswald animators had gone home. In this way *Plane Crazy* was completed by mid-May, almost before completion of the Oswald contract. Now Disney, armed with a sample reel, was ready to offer his new series to distributors.

Unfortunately, no distributor wanted it. The Disneys' first attempts to sell Mickey Mouse met with the same indifference as had the Laugh-O-grams and Arabian Nights. Still undaunted, Disney and his remaining crew plunged ahead with a second Mouse film. By now the Oswald animators had departed, and there was no need for secrecy within Disney's studio. The junior artists, passed over by Mintz's secret recruiting drive, were now available to assist Iwerks; the effect was that of an army consisting of one general and a handful of privates. (Of course, some of these lowly assistants — particularly Wilfred Jackson and Les Clark — would eventually hold positions of great importance at the Disney studio.)

Just as *Plane Crazy* had borrowed its inspiration from an earlier Oswald film, so the new picture, *Gallopin' Gaucho*, resorted to familiar territory. Mickey's visit to the cantina, his meeting with Minnie, her abduction by Pete, and Mickey's attempts to pursue them on his drunken ostrich were all borrowed from the 1927 cartoon *Harem Scarem*, in which Oswald had faced the same situation in the Arabian desert (with a camel instead of an ostrich). The climactic swordfight with Pete was strikingly reminiscent of a similar duel in *Alice on the Farm* (1925). And, of course, the setting and action were indebted to Douglas Fairbanks, whose adventures had inspired Julius the cat more than once. (Fairbanks' *The Gaucho* had premiered at Grauman's Chinese in November 1927, and was still in distribution when *Gallopin' Gaucho* was finished.)

Still, however, no one wanted Mickey Mouse. Disney was beginning to realize what a risk he had taken with his new independent stance; he had separated himself not only from Mintz but from Mintz's distribution channels. Despite the success of the Alice and Oswald series, Disney's name was not yet enough to sell a cartoon series by itself. No one had ever heard of Mickey Mouse; he was just another cartoon character. Disney's only chance was to find some gimmick to set his films apart from the rest.

The gimmick, of course, was sound. In the summer of 1928, even before *Gallopin' Gaucho* was finished, Disney, Iwerks and company began the experiments with sound which led to Mickey's breakthrough picture: *Steamboat Willie*. This film has already been widely praised for its innovative use of sound to create brilliant musical gags. But even these gags had roots in Disney's silent period. The most famous of them — the goat who swallows Minnie's banjo and the music to "Turkey in the Straw," and who "plays back" the song when she turns his tail like the crank of a hand organ — had appeared in practically identical form in the Oswald short *Rival Romeos*.

In the end, though it was sound that first attracted the public's attention to Mickey Mouse, it was Disney's visual and storytelling skills — developed and polished throughout the silent period — that sustained Mickey's extraordinary popularity. As if to bear this out, the two silent Mickeys were quickly outfitted with musical soundtracks. Once the character had been established, those two films were as eagerly accepted as any of the

Gallopin' Gaucho; below: *Steamboat Willie.* (Copyright Walt Disney Company)

Taking it to the limit. Walt and the Mickey Mouse tie-in phenomenon. (Copyright Walt Disney Company)

later "talking" Mickeys. The reviewer for *Variety* (9 June 1929, p. 10), writing of the sonorized *Gallopin' Gaucho*, made an astute point: "Sound effects won some laughs here on their own, but after it's all over the impression remains that any alert pit drummer can duplicate .... Value in this one comes from the antics Disney makes his figures perform ... good with or without sound."

The previous seven years had been a remarkable time for Disney. He had produced an exceptional body of work, and in the process had acquired a wealth of filmmaking skills and ideas. Now he and Roy were prepared to use those skills and ideas to achieve even greater triumphs. As they sailed *Steamboat Willie* into the future, they knew that nothing could hold them back.

WALT DISNEY SILENT FILMOGRAPHY (1921-1928)

The following is a complete list of the silent films made by Walt Disney and his collaborators. We have also included *Steamboat Willie*, Disney's first sound picture, because of its close affinities to the first two Mickeys. For credits and production information, we have relied primarily on copyright registration applications, payroll records, Disney business correspondence, and interviews with participants. We are particularly indebted to Rudy Ising, Friz Freleng, and Virginia Davis McGhee for sharing their files and personal recollections.

For summaries of lost films, we have drawn on plot synopses contained in copyright applications, the gag and situation summary sheets, and continuity drafts contained at the Disney archive. In the case of Oswald, we have also consulted story sketches, the marginalia written on character sketches, and synopses published in Universal's house organ, *Universal Weekly*. *Universal Weekly* is available at the American Museum of the Moving Image in Queens, New York.

The summaries for surviving films derive primarily from our own screenings. For making films available, we are grateful to the Walt Disney Company; the Museum of Modern Art; the Library of Congress; Film Preservation Associates; the British Film Institute, the Filmový Archive, Prague; DIF, Wiesbaden; and UCLA. Special thanks to Ginnie Davis McGhee and the Nederlands Filmmuseum for their extraordinary cooperation.

In a few instances, we were not able to view the films ourselves, and have relied on the eyewitness testimony of others. We acknowledge the generous assistance of Dave Smith, Livio Jacob, and Lorenzo Codelli. We are particularly grateful to collectors Jan Zaalberg and David Wyatt responsible for unearthing and sharing their unique prints of crucial Disney silents.

Several caveats to anyone using this list. The reader should keep in mind that although we assign specific credits to individuals, job classifications at Disney were very informal during the silent years. Disney expected all employees to pitch in and help with any phase of the work at any time. When the ink and paint department in the Hollywood studio was short-handed, for instance, Roy Disney occasionally helped paint cels. Rudolph Ising frequently doubled as camera operator and junior animator. Records were seldom kept of these random cross-overs, and so they are seldom recorded here.

We are also aware that after mid-1927 credits become appreciably skimpier as the Disney staff grows larger. The studio grew with the success of Oswald, and in July 1927 Disney divided his animators into units. At that point it becomes extremely difficult to determine who precisely worked on what, even though we have a full list of animators on the company payroll (see note on p. 152). Rather than speculate, we have curtailed credits, but the reader should be aware that as many as six or seven animators worked on late Oswalds.

Titles are listed in order of completion. Release dates for the Alice series represent the dates that Winkler Pictures and then FBO offered the films for release. They are *not* dates on which Alice films were originally screened. On at least two occasions, exhibitors declined to rent the Disney release, so the film was withdrawn, and then "re-released." Except when theater exhibition dates are noted, we make no claims for when individual Alice titles were actually exhibited. In the case of several late Oswalds we have been obliged to deduce release dates from publicity and copyright materials. Such dates are marked with an asterisk (*).

A key to the abbreviations for archival print sources is found at the end of the filmography.

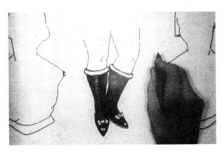

Frame enlargements from the *Newman Laugh-O-gram* sample reel. (Courtesy Carlo Montanaro)

DISNEY IN KANSAS CITY

NEWMAN LAUGH-O-GRAMS (sample reel, 1921)
Direction and animation: Walt Disney. Privately produced in the Disney garage at 3028 Bellefontaine Ave. Kansas City premiere at Newman Theater with *Mama's Affair* (First National) on 20 March 1921.

A lightning sketch artist (Disney) draws topical gags. Women's stockings move; Kansas City police are fired.

The Newman Laugh-O-grams were fillers inserted into *News and Views*, Newman's weekly newsreel that circulated among his three movie houses in Kansas City.

Print source/s: WDA 35mm; GLASS 16mm, FPA 16mm, CDF 16mm.

LITTLE RED RIDING HOOD (Laugh-O-gram, 1922)
Direction: Walt Disney. Animation: Walt Disney, Rudolph Ising, and others unknown. Produced at Disney garage at 3028 Bellefontaine Ave. ca. October 1921-May 1922. No theatrical or non-theatrical release.

Grandma makes doughnuts assisted by her cat, who loses all nine of its lives when it eats one. Red Riding Hood goes out for a run in her dog-propelled car and meets a top hatted "wolf" in his flivver. He hides in Grandma's house (she has gone off to the movies) and attacks when Red Riding Hood arrives. Just when all seems lost for the girl, a dashing hero (a human caricature) arrives by plane, dumps the villain in a handy lake, and flies off with Red Riding Hood into the sunset.

Print source/s: WYATT 16mm.

THE FOUR MUSICIANS OF BREMEN (Laugh-O-gram, 1922)
Direction: Walt Disney. Animation: Walt Disney, Rudolph Ising, and others unknown. Produced in the Disney garage at 3028 Bellefontaine Ave. ca. April-May 1922. Distributed non-theatrically by Pictorial Clubs Inc. of New York on regional circuit.

A band of itinerant musicians — a Donkey, Chicken, Dog, and Cat — are run out of town by an angry mob. At the side of a lake, the Cat devises a scheme to lure fish ashore. The scheme backfires when a furious swordfish emerges, and pursues the musicians into a tree trunk. The musicians fall into a cabin filled with masked bandits in Tyrolean hats. The bandits flee, but then lay siege to the house with shot and cannon. The Cat foils the bandits by riding a cannon ball and clubbing the bandits with a baseball bat.

Print source/s: WDA 35mm, NFA 35mm; MoMA 16mm, CDF 16mm.

JACK AND THE BEANSTALK (Laugh-O-gram, 1922)
Direction: Walt Disney. Animation: Walt Disney, Hugh Harman, Rudolph Ising, Carman "Max" Maxwell, Lorey Tague, Otto Walliman. Produced at Laugh-O-gram studio at 31st St, KC. ca. Spring-Summer 1922. Distributed non-theatrically by Pictorial Clubs Inc. of New York on regional circuit.

GOLDIE LOCKS AND THE THREE BEARS (Laugh-O-gram, 1922)
Direction: Walt Disney. Animation: Walt Disney, Hugh Harman, Rudolph Ising, Carman "Max" Maxwell, Lorey Tague, Otto Walliman. Camera: Red Lyon. Produced at Laugh-O-gram studio at 31st St, KC. ca. September-October 1922. No theatrical or non-theatrical release.

PUSS IN BOOTS (Laugh-O-gram, 1922)
Direction: Walt Disney. Animation: Walt Disney, Hugh Harman, Rudolph Ising, Carman "Max" Maxwell, Lorey Tague, Otto Walliman. Camera: Red Lyon. Produced at Laugh-O-gram studio at 31st St ca. September-October 1922. No theatrical or non-theatrical release.

A boy and his female cat scheme to win the hand of the princess of Kingville. Inspired by Rudolf Vaselino six-reeler called "Throwing the Bull," the boy enters a bull fight as a masked toreador, wins the contest and wins the sweetheart.

Print source/s: WDA 35mm, MTL 35mm, LoC 35mm, FPA 35mm; GLASS 16mm, FPA 16mm, CDF 16mm.

Title card for a surviving Laugh-O-gram.

CINDERELLA (Laugh-O-gram, 1922)
Direction: Walt Disney. Animation: Walt Disney, Ubbe Iwerks, Hugh Harman, Rudolph Ising, Carman "Max" Maxwell, Lorey Tague, Otto Walliman. Camera: Red Lyon. Produced at Laugh-O-gram studio at 31st St, KC. October-November 1922. No theatrical or non-theatrical release.

A comic, updated version of the Grimms' fairytale. The ugly sisters read "Beauty Secrets" and "Eat and Grow Thin," while the Prince is introduced pursuing a bear in a royal hunt. The Fairy Godmother provides Cinderella a posh car instead of a coach, attended by a cat.

Print source/s: WYATT 16mm.

TOMMY TUCKER'S TOOTH
Produced by Laugh-O-gram Films for Dr. Thomas B. McCrum. Non-theatrical distribution to the Missouri school system. Produced December 1922.

Direction: Walt Disney. Camera: Walt Pfeiffer.

John W. Records (Jimmie Jones).

Live-action, with animated sequence. Tommy Tucker, who takes good care of his teeth, is contrasted with the sluggard Jimmie Jones. When the boys apply for a job, Tommy gets the job because of his personal appearance. Jimmie learns his lesson, and after improving his appearance, returns for a second interview.

Print source/s: WDA 35mm; NLM 16mm.

"LAFFLETS" (privately produced/Laugh-O-gram, 1922-1923)
A series that combined cartoon and stop-motion material. Each issue approximately 300 feet long. Titles:
GOLF IN SLOW MOTION
DESCHA'S TRYST WITH THE MOON
AESTHETIC CAMPING
REUBEN'S BIG DAY
RESCUED
A STAR PITCHER
THE WOODLAND POTTER
A PIRATE FOR A DAY
Direction: Walt Disney. Animation: Walt Disney, Rudolph Ising, Ubbe Iwerks, and unnamed others. Edited by Aletha Reynolds.

Produced in the Disney garage at 3028 Bellefontaine Ave. ca. April-May 1922, and at the Laugh-O-gram studio ca. November 1922-April 1923.

MARTHA (Song-O-Reel, 1923)

Direction: Walt Disney. Camera: Red Lyon. Produced at Laugh-O-gram offices, and at various Kansas City locations, in spring 1923.

A sing-along short based on the song "Martha: Just a Plain Old Fashioned Name," by Joe L. Sanders. Produced for Jenkins Music Company for screening at the Isis Theater, Kansas City.

ALICE'S WONDERLAND

Produced at Laugh-O-gram studio at 3239 Troost Ave in spring 1923. Delivered ca. 14 October 1923. Distributed non-theatrically by Pictorial Clubs Inc. of New York on regional circuit. Copyrighted as ALICE IN SLUMBERLAND by Pathé Exchange Inc. 29 September 1926 MU3592.

Direction and scenario: Walt Disney. Camera: Ubbe Iwerks, Rudolph Ising. Technical direction: Hugh Harman, Carman "Max" Maxwell.

Virginia Davis (Alice), Walt Disney (animator), Mrs. Margaret Davis (Alice's mother), Ubbe Iwerks, Hugh Harman, Rudolph Ising (other animators).

Animation with live action frame story. Alice visits a cartoon studio where she watches animated characters spring off a drawing board. A dog chases his dog house; a mouse torments a cat. Animators gather around and interact with the cartoons. That night, Alice dreams she has taken a trip to Cartoonland. At an outdoor party, Alice entertains the animals with a specialty dance. Rampaging lions, escaped from the Cartoonland zoo, break up the party and chase Alice. She awakens from a bad dream.

Print source/s: WDA 35mm (slightly abridged).

Alice's Wonderland.
(Courtesy Walt Disney Company)

DISNEY IN HOLLYWOOD

"ALICE COMEDIES"

ALICE'S DAY AT SEA

Produced by M. J. Winkler Productions; states rights distribution. Shipped ca. 15 December 1923. Not copyrighted. Release: 1 March 1924.

Direction, story, animation: Walt Disney. Live-action camera: Roy Disney. Edited by Margaret Winkler.

Animated at a small office at 4651 Kingswell Ave. Partially remade January 1925 with new animation by Ubbe Iwerks, Rollin "Ham" Hamilton, Thurston Harper.

Virginia Davis (Alice), Peggy the German shepherd (dog).

Live-action frame story: Alice's dog drives his mistress to the Santa Monica shore in a kid's racing car. There Alice meets an old sea salt who recounts how his sailing ship foundered in a storm. A short animated sequence dramatizes the shipwreck. Alice falls asleep and dreams that she has drowned. Animated narrative: At the bottom of the sea, Alice finds a zoo of underwater animals including a "cat fish" family, a "sea lion," and an elephant. A whale swallows her; she escapes the whale only to be caught in the tentacles of a giant octopus.

Print source/s: PRA 35mm, AMS 35mm (as ALICE WIL ZEEMAN WORDEN).

ALICE HUNTING IN AFRICA

Produced by M. J. Winkler Productions; states rights distribution. In production December 1923; shipped ca. 21 January 1924. Not copyrighted. Release: 15 November 1924. Direction, story, animation: Walt Disney. Live-action camera: Roy Disney. Edited by Margaret Winkler.

Virginia Davis (Alice).

From atop a donkey, safari hunter Alice chases a bear; then, on a camel's back, she joins up with her cat Julius, who is riding an elephant. Julius shoots at a sleeping hippopotamus and then at an eagle, denuding him of feathers; he cavorts with his elephant, until the elephant is frightened by a mouse. While Alice chases the mouse, Julius continues to fire at more animals — a lion, a giraffe, and a cheetah — until finally a mother cheetah turns on him.

Note: Synopsis taken from revised print. The live action was shot in rented vacant lot at Hollywood Blvd and Rodney Drive. Ca. October 1924, live action prolog deleted and animation partially revised by Ubbe Iwerks, Rollin "Ham" Hamilton, and Thurston Harper.

Print source/s: PRA 35mm (1924 revised print as ALICE V AFRICE).

ALICE'S SPOOKY ADVENTURE

Produced by M. J. Winkler Productions; states rights distribution. Shipped 22 February 1924. Not copyrighted. Release: 1 April 1924.

Direction/story: Walt Disney. Animation: Walt Disney, Rollin "Ham" Hamilton. Live-action camera: Roy Disney. Edited by Margaret Winkler.

Virginia Davis (Alice), Leon Holmes (tubby boy), "Spec" O'Donnell.

Live-action frame story: Sandlot baseball pitcher Alice enters an abandoned house to retrieve a lost baseball and is knocked unconscious by falling plaster. Animation: In a dream city called Spookville, Alice and an unnamed black cat attend an open air concert performed by musical ghosts. Ghosts spot the intruders and give chase. Awakened by a black cat licking her hand, Alice leaves the house, is spotted by a policeman, and is thrown in jail.

Print source/s: WDA 35mm (incomplete), NFA 35mm, AMS 35mm (as ALICE IN HET SPOOKHUIS).

ALICE'S WILD WEST SHOW

Produced by M. J. Winkler Productions; states rights distribution. In production February 1924; shipped ca. 28 March 1924. Not copyrighted. Release: 1 May 1924.

Direction/story: Walt Disney. Animation: Walt Disney, Rollin "Ham" Hamilton. Ink and paint: Lillian Bounds, Kathleen Dollard. Edited by Margaret Winkler.

Virginia Davis (Alice), Leon Holmes (Tubby O'Brien), and Tommy Hicks.

Live-action frame story: Alice and the gang put on a Wild West show and must contend with a heckling bully and his gang who take over the front row. Alice entertains with a series of tall tales: how as driver of a stagecoach she outfoxed marauding Indians; and how as sheriff she pursued a safe robber. Kids boo Alice; losing patience, she jumps off stage and pursues the chief heckler and pummels him.

Two frame enlargements from *Alice's Day at Sea*. (Courtesy Nederlands Filmmuseum)

Alice's Spooky Adventure; below,
Alice's Wild West Show. (Courtesy
Nederlands Filmmuseum)

Frame enlargement from *Alice's Fishy Story.* (Courtesy Nederlands Filmmuseum).
Below: Lobby card for *Alice and the Dog Catcher.* (Courtesy Walt Disney Company)

Print source/s: WDA 35mm, AMS 35mm (as ALICE IN HET WILDE WESTEN).

ALICE'S FISHY STORY

Produced by M. J. Winkler Productions; states rights distribution. In production April 1924. Los Angeles preview at Bard's Hollywood Theatre May 1924. Shipped 7 May 1924. Not copyrighted. Release: 1 June 1924.

Direction/story: Walt Disney. Animation: Walt Disney, Rollin "Ham" Hamilton. Ink and paint: Lillian Bounds, Kathleen Dollard. Edited by Margaret Winkler.

Virginia Davis (Alice), Leon Holmes (tubby fishing pal), Walt Disney (auto driver), Peggy the German shepherd (Alice's dog), Tommy Hicks.

Live-action frame story: Alice abandons piano practice to join her pals at the fishing hole. While waiting for the fish to bite, Alice tells an animated tall tale: how she caught a huge fish in the North Pole. Alice and her cat learn that the fish in Eskimo Land are on strike, threatening the Eskimos with starvation. The cat saves the day with his ingenious plan: he feeds the fish chewing tobacco, and clubs them when they surface to spit.

Print source/s: WDA 35mm, NFA 35mm (nearly complete), AMS 35mm (tinted Dutch release print ALICE GAAT UIT HENGELEN).

ALICE AND THE DOG CATCHER

Produced by M. J. Winkler Productions; states rights distribution. In production April 1924. Los Angeles premiere at Bard's Hollywood Theatre. Delivered 3 June 1924. Not copyrighted. Release: 1 July 1924.

Direction/story: Walt Disney. Animation: Walt Disney, Rollin "Ham" Hamilton. Ink and paint: Lillian Bounds, Kathleen Dollard. Live-action camera: Harry Forbes.

Virginia Davis (Alice), Leon Holmes, Joe Allen, Tommy Hicks, Peggy the German shepherd.

Live-action frame story: In the gang's clubhouse, Alice presides over a secret society that learns about two dog catchers lurking in the neighborhood. Alice's animated tale of dogs trapped and thrown into a penitentiary stir the gang to action. The clubhouse dog frees impounded dogs, Alice helps steal the dog catcher's truck, and the truck goes berserk racing through Los Angeles before crashing down a hill.

The last of the six Alices specified in the original Disney-Winkler contract.

Print source/s: AMS 35mm (as ALICE EN DE HONDENVANGERS).

Alice the Peacemaker.
(Courtesy Nederlands Filmmuseum)

ALICE THE PEACEMAKER

Produced by M. J. Winkler Productions; states rights distribution. In production June-July 1924. Los Angeles preview at Bard's Hollywood Theater. Not copyrighted. Release: 1 August 1924.

Direction/story: Walt Disney. Animation: Ubbe Iwerks, Rollin "Ham" Hamilton. Ink and paint: Lillian Bounds, Kathleen Dollard. Animation camera: Mike Marcus. Live-action camera: Harry Forbes.

Virginia Davis (Alice), Leon Holmes (tubby newsboy), "Spec" O'Donnell (freckle-faced newsboy).

Live-action frame: Alice breaks up a fight between two rival newsboys, telling them a cautionary animated tale about a battling cat and mouse. Ike the Mouse and Mike the Cat are feuding thieves: they fight as they steal food from a refrigerator. Alice gets them to reconcile, but a poster announces a reward for their capture. A police dog chases them; Alice with the help of a mule and an ingenious plan outwits the cop.

Print source/s: WDA 35mm, AMS 35mm (as ALICE IN KAMERAADSCHAFT).

ALICE GETS IN DUTCH

Produced by M. J. Winkler Productions; states rights distribution. In production August 1924. Los Angeles preview at Bard's Hollywood Theater August 1924. Delivered 27 August 1924. Not copyrighted. NYC premiere at Piccadilly Theater 20 October 1924 with *This Woman* (Warner Bros.). Release: 1 November 1924.

Animation: Ubbe Iwerks, Rollin "Ham" Hamilton. Ink and paint: Lillian Bounds, Kathleen Dollard. Animation camera: Mike Marcus. Live-action camera: Harry Forbes. Edited by George Winkler.

Virginia Davis (Alice), "Spec" O'Donnell, Leon Holmes, David F. Hollander (boy with dark hair), Marjorie Sewell (one of the school children), Mrs. Hunt (teacher), Peggy the German shepherd (dog).

Live-action frame story: Schoolgirl Alice is forced to sit in a corner wearing a dunce cap after misbehaving. She falls asleep and dreams an animated dream. She and her three friends — a cat, a pup, and a donkey — dance and sing, but their fun is interrupted by an old-maid school teacher and three walking schoolbooks. The friends declare war: the teacher and books fire cannon shot; Alice's gang retaliates with a cannon made in a junkyard. They fire "Cheyenne Pepper" and reduce the enemy to sneezing helplessness.

Print source/s: WDA 35mm, PRA 35mm.

ALICE AND THE THREE BEARS

Produced by M. J. Winkler Productions; states rights distribution. Los Angeles preview at Bard's Hollywood Theater ca. 25 September 1924. Shipped 27 September 1924. Not copyrighted. Release: 1 December 1924.

Animation: Ubbe Iwerks, Rollin "Ham" Hamilton. Ink and paint: Lillian Bounds, Kathleen Dollard. Camera: Mike Marcus. Edited by George Winkler.

Virginia Davis (Alice).

Bears, brewing moonshine, need more hops. Little Bear is sent to the pond where he collects "hops" from leaping frogs. Enter, on a scooter, Alice and her cat, inadvertently discovering the bears' hideout. The cat fights Little Bear, then Ma and Pa. Leaving the cat for dead, the Bears take Alice to a sawmill and strap her to a deadly conveyor belt. The cat, summoning his nine lives, watches as eight of them are overpowered by the bears. He saves his ninth by administering moonshine, and rescues Alice.

Print source/s: WDA 35mm, NFA 35mm.

Above: Filming *Alice and the Dog Catcher*. (Courtesy Walt Disney Company)
Left: Virginia Davis as Alice reads a fairy tale to Julius the cat as the animated bears sneak up behind. Lobby card for the 1924 cartoon *Alice and the Three Bears*. (Courtesy Virginia Davis McGhee)

ALICE THE PIPER

Produced by M. J. Winkler Productions; states rights distribution. In production September-October 1924; delivered 1 November 1924. Los Angeles preview at Bard's Hollywood Theater 2 November 1924. Not copyrighted. Release: 15 December 1924.

Animation: Ubbe Iwerks, Rollin "Ham" Hamilton, Thurston Harper. Ink and paint: Lillian Bounds, Kathleen Dollard. Animation camera: Mike Marcus. Live-action camera: Harry Forbes.

Virginia Davis (Alice).

The king of "Hamlin," tormented by mice, posts a reward for anyone who can drive them off. Alice and her cat, two hoboes, take on the job. They play the fife and fiddle, but their music only entertains the mice — it does not lure them to the river. They finally succeed with a gigantic vacuum cleaner found in a nearby junkyard, but when the king pays them only five dollars, they vacuum him up, along with his house and belongings.

Print source/s: WDA 35mm (incomplete), PRA 35mm, AMS 35mm (as ALICE VANGT MUIZEN, tinted).

ALICE CANS THE CANNIBALS

Produced by M. J. Winkler Productions; states rights distribution. In production November 1924; shipped 29 November 1924. Not copyrighted. Release: 1 January 1925. Plays Los Angeles at the Criterion for two weeks starting 7 March 1925 with *The Last Laugh.*

Animation: Ubbe Iwerks, Rollin "Ham" Hamilton, Thurston Harper. Ink and paint: Lillian Bounds, Kathleen Dollard. Camera: Mike Marcus. Edited by George Winkler.

Virginia Davis (Alice).

Alice and her cat crash their car into the ocean and after assorted adventures with fish and birds, find themselves marooned on a cannibal island. A cannibal chief and his tribesmen pursue them; by tossing ostrich eggs, hurling boulders from rubber trees, and firing a harpoon, the duo escape.

Print source/s: WDA 35mm, MTL 35mm, LoC 35mm; GLASS 16mm, CDF 16mm.

ALICE THE TOREADOR

Produced by M. J. Winkler Productions; states rights distribution. In production November-December 1924; delivered 31 December 1924. Not copyrighted. Release: 15 January 1925.

Animation: Ubbe Iwerks, Rollin "Ham" Hamilton, Thurston Harper. Ink and paint: Lillian Bounds, Kathleen Dollard. Camera: Mike Marcus. Edited by George Winkler.

Virginia Davis (Alice).

Toreador Alice enters a bull fight competition, certain of winning after locating a docile, sleepy bull. Her scheme sours, however, when a rival cat named Terrible Tom switches her bull with a fiery animal he has coaxed off a billboard advertisement. Terrible Tom fights Alice's docile bull, but the animal turns ferocious after being hurled onto cactus and chases Terrible Tom out of the ring. Alice is chased by Tom's fiery bull, but Alice's cat saves the day when he lures him out of the ring, disguises himself as a bull, and lets Alice win the match.

Print source/s: WDA 35mm; LoC 16mm, GLASS 16mm, CDF 16mm.

ALICE GETS STUNG

Produced by M. J. Winkler Productions; states rights distribution. In production January 1925; completed and shipped 31 January 1925. Not copyrighted. Release: unknown (ca. March 1925).

Animation: Ubbe Iwerks, Rollin "Ham" Hamilton, Thurston Harper. Ink and paint: Lillian Bounds, Kathleen Dollard. Camera: Mike Marcus. Live-action camera: Phil Tannura.

Virginia Davis (Alice).

Julius pursues and captures a female rabbit, but releases her when she pleads for mercy in the name of her children. He resumes the chase — down a rabbit tunnel and on top a surging column of water — when he realizes he has been played for a fool. Alice and Julius encounter a bear jamboree. Alice playfully shoots at the animals, whereupon one infuriated bear chases the intruders away.

Print source/s: WDA 35mm (incomplete).

ALICE SOLVES THE PUZZLE

Produced by M. J. Winkler Productions; states rights distribution. In production February 1925; completed 27 February 1925. Release: 12 July 1925. NYC premiere at Rivoli Theater 24 March 1925 with *Sackcloth and Scarlet* (Paramount). Copyright M. J. Winkler 12 July 1925 MP3202.

Animation: Ubbe Iwerks, Rollin "Ham" Hamilton, Thurston Harper. Ink and paint: Lillian Bounds, Kathleen Dollard. Camera: Mike Marcus.

Margie Gay (Alice).

While Julius and Alice swim and dive on the shore, Bootleg Pete ("One-Eyed Pete" in the copyright registration) and his pelican sidekick sneak bootleg liquor past a patrolling coast guard dog. Pete gets Julius drunk on his liquor, then sneaks off to steal a crossword puzzle from Alice. Pete chases Alice to a lighthouse; her cries awaken Julius from his dreams; together they chase Pete away.

All shots relating to bootlegging and Julius' intoxication were deleted when the film was reissued.

Print source/s: WDA 35mm (reissue print), DIF 35mm (tinted); GLASS 16mm (reissue print), FPA 16mm (reissue print), CDF 16mm (reissue print).

ALICE'S EGG PLANT

Produced by M. J. Winkler Productions; states rights distribution. In production March 1925 as "Chicken Picture;" completed 27 March 1925. Los Angeles preview at Paramount Theater. Not copyrighted. NYC debut at Rivoli Theater 17 May 1925 with *Welcome Home* (Paramount).

Animation: Ubbe Iwerks, Rollin "Ham" Hamilton, Thurston Harper. Ink and paint: Lillian Bounds, Kathleen Dollard. Camera: Mike Marcus.

Dawn O'Day aka Anne Shirley (Alice).

Julius, the overseer of Alice's poultry farm, has an order to deliver 5,000 eggs to Skinem and Soakem, but a Bolshevik agitator (a rooster named Little Red Henski) persuades the hens to strike. To raise the necessary eggs, Alice sponsors a prize fight and

Alice's Egg Plant.

charges each customer one egg as the price of admission.

Print source/s: WDA 35mm, UCLA 35mm, MTL 35mm, MoMA 35mm, LoC 35mm; GLASS 16mm, FPA 16mm, CDF 16mm.

ALICE LOSES OUT

Produced by M. J. Winkler Productions; states rights distribution. In production April 1925; delivered 20 April 1925. Not copyrighted. Release: 1925.

Animation: Ubbe Iwerks, Rollin "Ham" Hamilton, Thurston Harper. Ink and paint: Lillian Bounds. Camera: Mike Marcus. Edited by George Winkler.

Margie Gay (Alice).

Alice runs a hotel that caters to its animal clientele with Julius doing all the work. Julius scrubs the floors, and when a wealthy pig registers, works as the hotel porter, the hotel barber, and the female manicurist. The pig flirts with the manicurist and gives chase when he discovers Julius' true gender.

Print source/s: WDA 35mm.

ALICE [GETS] STAGE STRUCK

Produced by M. J. Winkler Productions; states rights distribution. In production April-May 1925 as "Alice's Uncle Tom's Cabin;" completed 14 May 1925; delivered 29 May 1925. Not copyrighted. NYC premiere at Rivoli Theater 23 June 1925 with *The Light of Western Stars* (Paramount).

Animation: Ubbe Iwerks, Rollin "Ham" Hamilton, Thurston Harper. Ink and paint: Lillian Bounds. Camera: Mike Marcus. Edited by George Winkler.

Margie Gay (Alice), Leon Holmes, Joe Allen, Marjorie Sewell.

Live action frame story: Alice and the gang stage an Our Gang-style *Uncle Tom's Cabin* show. Playing the part of Little Eva, Alice is accidentally knocked out, and dreams herself in snowland with Julius, who is building a snowman. They run afoul of Pete the Bear who chases them into a winter cabin and across ice floes.

The main title of the sound reissue reads *Alice Gets Stage Struck*, but studio records from 1925 give the title simply as *Alice Stage Struck*.

Print source/s: WDA 35mm, LoC 35mm.

ALICE WINS THE DERBY

Produced by M. J. Winkler Productions; states rights distribution. In production May-June 1925; completed and delivered 9 June 1925. Copyright M. J. Winkler 5 May 1925 MP3203. NYC premiere at Piccadilly Theater 12 July 1925 with *The Woman Hater* (Warner Bros.).

Animation: Ubbe Iwerks, Rollin "Ham" Hamilton, Thurston Harper. Ink and paint: Lillian Bounds, Kathleen Dollard, Hazelle Linston. Camera: Mike Marcus. Edited by George Winkler.

Margie Gay (Alice).

Julius and Alice enter a cross-country auto race, but their car is sidetracked by false detours that villainous Pete the bear sets up. Finally Julius discovers a mechanical horse and rides it to victory in the steeplechase.

Print source/s: WDA 35mm, LoC 35mm.

ALICE PICKS THE CHAMP

Produced by M. J. Winkler Productions; states rights distribution. In production 28 May-17 June 1925 (animation); completed 1 July 1925. Los Angeles preview at Apollo Theater ca. July 1925. Not copyrighted.

Animation: Ubbe Iwerks, Rollin "Ham" Hamilton, Thurston Harper. Ink and paint: Ruth Disney, Irene Hamilton, Hazelle Linston. Camera: Mike Marcus. Edited by George Winkler.

When Tough Pete the boxing champ advertises for a sparring partner, Julius visits the gym, watches as Pete fights and destroys his other would-be partners in the ring. Prodded by Alice, Julius fights Pete, and after a comic fight that ends in the partial destruction of the ring, Julius wins.

Print source/s: WDA 35mm (incomplete), AMS 35mm.

Alice Picks the Champ.
(Courtesy Nederlands Filmmuseum)

ALICE'S TIN PONY

Produced by M. J. Winkler Productions; states rights distribution. In production

18 June-14 July 1925 (animation); completed 23 July 1925. Not copyrighted. NYC premiere at Warner's Theater 20 September 1925 with *Below the Line* (Warner Bros.).

Animation: Ubbe Iwerks, Rollin "Ham" Hamilton, Thurston Harper, Hugh Harman, Rudolph Ising. Ink and paint: Ruth Disney, Irene Hamilton, Hazelle Linston, Walker Harman. Camera: Rudolph Ising. Edited by George Winkler.

Margie Gay (Alice).

Alice and Julius, locomotive engineers on a passenger train, transport a large payroll shipment that attracts the attention of the Bear and his gang. Alice and Julius foil the gang's various schemes to rob the train.

Print source/s: WDA 35mm, UCLA 35mm, MoMA 35mm (incomplete); GLASS 16mm, FPA 16mm, CDF 16mm.

ALICE CHOPS THE SUEY

Produced by M. J. Winkler Productions; states rights distribution. In production 15-31 July 1925 (animation); completed 8 August; shipped 18 August 1925. Not copyrighted. Los Angeles preview at Bards Hollywood Theater 17 August 1925. 600 ft.

Animation: Ubbe Iwerks, Rollin "Ham" Hamilton, Thurston Harper, Hugh Harman, Rudolph Ising. Ink and paint: Ruth Disney, Irene Hamilton, Hazelle Linston, Walker Harman. Camera: Rudolph Ising. Hand photo: Rees Bros. Edited by George Winkler.

Margie Gay (Alice).

Alice and Julius spring to life from an ink bottle; an evil jinn kidnaps Alice and trundles her off in a bag to Chinatown. Julius, in mad pursuit, disguises himself as a Chinaman, eventually retrieves the bag with Alice inside it, and runs away on unicycle. The jinn and his accomplices give chase. Alice and Julius escape by jumping back into the inkwell.

Print source/s: WDA 35mm; LoC 16mm (with an incorrect main title, "Felix in Chinatown"), GLASS 16mm, CDF 16mm.

ALICE THE JAIL BIRD

Produced by M. J. Winkler Productions; states rights distribution. In production 30 July (live action) and 1-22 August (animation); completed 29 August 1925. Not copyrighted. Los Angeles preview at Paramount Theater 1 September 1925. Release: 15 September 1925.

Animation: Ubbe Iwerks, Rollin "Ham" Hamilton, Thurston Harper, Hugh Harman, Rudolph Ising. Ink and paint: Ruth Disney, Irene Hamilton, Hazelle Linston, Walker Harman. Camera: Rudolph Ising.

Margie Gay (Alice)

Alice and Julius, riding a turtle, steal a pie and run from the police. Tricked into entering a paddy wagon, they are transported to a chain gang where they pound rocks. In a prison yard, an ostrich helps them engineer their escape.

Print source/s: WDA 35mm; MoMA 16mm, LoC 16mm (as "The Jail Break"), GLASS 16mm, CDF 16mm.

ALICE PLAYS CUPID

Produced by M. J. Winkler Productions; states rights distribution. In production 24 August-9 September 1925 as "Alice in Love;" completed 17 September 1925. Not copyrighted. Los Angeles preview at Apollo Theater 18 September 1925. Release: 15 October 1925.

Animation: Ubbe Iwerks, Rollin "Ham" Hamilton, Thurston Harper, Hugh Harman, Rudolph Ising. Ink and paint: Ruth Disney, Irene Hamilton, Hazelle Linston, Walker Harman. Camera: Rudolph Ising.

Margie Gay (Alice).

Julius the lifeguard falls in love with a flirtatious female cat. He rescues her from drowning, then retrieves her hat by fighting a bass for it at the bottom of the sea. That night, he serenades her with his banjo, much to the annoyance of her father. The two cats elope in a getaway car driven by Alice, and some time later parade their troupe of kittens past an astonished Alice.

Print source/s: WDA 35mm; MoMA 16mm.

ALICE RATTLED BY RATS

Produced by M. J. Winkler Productions; states rights distribution. In production 10-26 September 1925 (animation); completed 6 October 1925. Not copyrighted. Los Angeles preview at Apollo Theater 9 October 1925. Release: 15 November 1925.

Animation: Ubbe Iwerks, Rollin "Ham" Hamilton, Thurston Harper, Hugh Harman, Rudolph Ising. Ink and paint: Ruth Disney, Irene Hamilton, Hazelle Linston, Walker Harman. Camera: Rudolph Ising.

Margie Gay (Alice).

Left to protect Alice's house, Julius soon falls into a liquor still in the basement and drinks himself into oblivion. The rats, free to play, entertain themselves by dancing, playing phonograph records, cavorting with the player piano, and using the bathtub for a swimming pool.

Print source/s: WDA 35mm, UCLA 35mm; GLASS 16mm, FPA 16mm, CDF 16mm.

ALICE IN THE JUNGLE

Produced by M. J. Winkler Productions; states rights distribution. Partially revised from ALICE HUNTING IN AFRICA, in production December 1923. Animated 28 September-14 October 1925; completed 21 October 1925. Not copyrighted. Los Angeles preview at Iris Theater 23 October 1925. Release: 15 December 1925.

Animation: Ubbe Iwerks, Rollin "Ham" Hamilton, Thurston Harper, Hugh Harman, Rudolph Ising. Ink and paint: Ruth Disney, Irene Hamilton, Hazelle Linston, Walker Harman. Camera: Rudolph Ising.

Virginia Davis (Alice).

Safari hunters Alice and Julius encounter wild animals as they wander through the jungle on an elephant's back. A schoolkid hippo eats a barber shop pole; Julius replaces it with a tiger's tail. Alice plays with a lion cub and his chased by the father. Julius saves her, but the two of them are then chased by a pack of lions. A flying elephant intervenes and saves them both.

Title given in studio records as "Alice in the Jungles."

Print source/s: WDA 35mm, BAR 35mm; GLASS 16mm, FPA 16mm, CDF 16mm; private collection 9.5mm (incomplete, as GIGOTO SUR LE SEUIL DE LA JUNGLE).

ALICE ON THE FARM

Produced by M. J. Winkler Productions; states rights distribution. In production 15 October-2 November 1925 (animation); completed 7 November 1925. Not copyrighted. Los Angeles preview at Bard's Glendale Theater 11 November 1925. Release: 1 January 1926.

Animation: Ubbe Iwerks, Rollin "Ham" Hamilton, Thurston Harper, Hugh Harman, Rudolph Ising. Ink and paint: Irene Hamilton, Hazelle Linston, Walker Harman. Camera: Rudolph Ising.

Margie Gay (Alice).

Julius on Alice's farm finds ingenious ways to summon and milk his musical cow. The Bear kidnaps Alice; Julius pursues them on a saw horse; duels with the Bear in a small cabin and immobilizes him with a bucket of starch.

Print source/s: WDA 35mm, UCLA 35mm, LoC 35mm; GLASS 16mm, FPA 16mm, CDF 16mm.

ALICE'S BALLOON RACE

Produced by M. J. Winkler Productions; states rights distribution. In production 3 November-10 December 1925 (animation); completed 11 December 1925. Los Angeles preview at Bard's Glendale Theater 11 December 1925. Shipped 13 December 1925. Not copyrighted. Release: 15 January 1926.

Animation: Ubbe Iwerks, Rollin "Ham" Hamilton, Thurston Harper, Hugh Harman, Rudolph Ising. Ink and paint: Ruth Disney, Irene Hamilton, Hazelle Linston, Walker Harman. Camera: Rudolph Ising.

Margie Gay (Alice).

Julius and Alice have entered an air balloon race, pitted against the evil Bear, a white terrier, and other assorted animals. A gigantic sneeze from Hippo sets them off; the gags that mark the race involve Julius' trying to keep aloft as his balloon suffers from various puncturations.

Print source/s: WDA 35mm, LoC 35mm; GLASS 16mm, CDF 16mm.

ALICE'S ORPHAN

Alice's Orphan.

Produced by M. J. Winkler Productions; states rights distribution. In production November-14 December 1925 (animation); completed 19 December 1925. Los Angeles preview at Bard's Glendale Theater 22 December 1925. Not copyrighted. Release: January-February 1926.

Animation: Ubbe Iwerks, Rollin "Ham" Hamilton, Thurston Harper, Hugh Harman, Rudolph Ising. Ink and paint: Ruth Disney, Irene Hamilton, Hazelle Linston, Walker Harman. Camera: Rudolph Ising.

Margie Gay (Alice).

Julius finds an abandoned baby at the edge of a skating pond; he takes it home and, as a bachelor father, suffers various misadventures trying to take care of it. He gives the baby, named Oscar, a bath; teaches Oscar table manners, and tries to make him go to sleep.

The title is given in studio records as *Alice's Ornery Orphan,* but the original main title reads simply *Alice's Orphan.*

Print source/s: WDA 35mm; MoMA 16mm, GLASS 16mm, FPA 16mm, CDF 16mm.

ALICE'S LITTLE PARADE

Produced by M. J. Winkler Productions; states rights distribution. In production December 1925-January 1926; completed 13 January. Los Angeles preview at Iris Theater. Shipped 14 January 1926. Not copyrighted. Release: 1 February 1926.

Animation: Ubbe Iwerks, Rollin "Ham" Hamilton, Thurston Harper, Hugh Harman, Rudolph Ising. Ink and paint: Ruth Disney, Irene Hamilton, Walker Harman. Camera: Rudolph Ising.

Margie Gay (Alice)

War is declared: Julius raises the alarm a la Paul Revere and joins the all-animal army to fight the mice. Wounded in action (first his head is blown off, then he loses his leg), he is repaired in the parts department of a military hospital. Finally, he decoys the mice with cheese and defeats them singlehanded.

ALICE'S MYSTERIOUS MYSTERY

Produced by M. J. Winkler Productions; states rights distribution. In production January 1926; shipped 3 February 1926. Not copyrighted. Release: 15 February 1926.

Animation: Ubbe Iwerks, Rollin "Ham" Hamilton, Hugh Harman, Rudolph Ising. Ink and paint: Ruth Disney, Irene Hamilton, Walker Harman. Camera: Rudolph Ising.

Margie Gay (Alice).

Alice and Julius, detectives, are hired to trace missing puppies. The youngsters are being kidnapped en masse by the evil Bear and his sidekick rodent, who steal them away from school, take them to an underground prison, and have them ground up into hot dog sausages. When Alice and Julius see the scheme in action, they trick the Bear to fall into his own trap, and liberate the puppies.

Print source/s: WDA 35mm; HABER 16mm.

ALICE CHARMS THE FISH

Produced by Winkler Pictures Inc; distributed by FBO. In production March 1926; Los Angeles preview at Bard's Hollywood Theater 19 April 1926. Delivered 29 April 1926. Negative cost: $1,529.30. Copyright R-C Pictures Corp 28 June 1926 LP22845. Release: 6 September 1926.

Animation: Ubbe Iwerks, Rollin "Ham" Hamilton, Hugh Harman, Rudolph Ising. Ink and paint: Irene Hamilton, Walker Harman. Camera: Rudolph Ising.

Margie Gay (Alice).

Alice and Julius fish in a lake in order to stock their fish market. Alice lures fish ashore with her flute and the two pals try various comic ploys to trap them on shore. Fish escape from an ice box, knock Alice and Julius cold, and flee back to the water.

First film completed in new Disney studio at 2719 Hyperion.

ALICE IN THE WOOLY WEST

Produced by Winkler Pictures Inc.; distributed by FBO. In production January-February 1926; delivered 31 March 1926. Copyright R-C Pictures Corp 4 October 1926 LP23197. Release: 4 October 1926.

Animation: Ubbe Iwerks, Rollin "Ham" Hamilton, Hugh Harman, Rudolph Ising. Ink and paint: Ruth Disney, Irene Hamilton, Walker Harman. Camera: Rudolph Ising.

Margie Gay (Alice).

Alice is among the passengers robbed when Bear Bandit and his gang of mice hold up a stage coach. When the Bear kidnaps Alice, Julius rides to the rescue.

Print source/s: WDA 35mm, MTL 35mm, AMS 35mm (as ALICE WORDT GEKIDNAPT; main title incorrectly identifies film as a Mickey Mouse called TARABOEM).

Alice in the Wooly West.
(Courtesy Nederlands Filmmuseum)

ALICE'S MONKEY BUSINESS

Produced by Winkler Pictures Inc.; distributed by FBO. In production February-March 1926. Los Angeles preview at Iris Theater 25 March 1926; delivered 20 April 1926. Negative cost: $1,661.88. Copyright R-C Pictures Corp 18 September 1926 LP23198. Release: 20 September 1926.

Animation: Ubbe Iwerks, Rollin "Ham" Hamilton, Hugh Harman, Rudolph Ising. Ink and paint: Ruth Disney, Irene Hamilton, Walker Harman. Camera: Rudolph Ising.

Margie Gay (Alice).

Big game hunters Alice and Julius find themselves pursued by a pair of jungle tigers they had sought to capture. Brought before a King Lion in his court, the duo are sentenced to expulsion by a swift drop-kick. They retaliate by directing a swarm of fleas to attack the king and his court.

ALICE THE FIRE FIGHTER

Produced by Winkler Pictures Inc; distributed by FBO. In production April-May 1926. Negative cost: $1,519. Los Angeles preview at Bard's Hollywood Theater 12 May 1926; delivered 18 May 1926. Copyright R-C Pictures Corp 18 October 1926 LP23310. Release: 18 October 1926.

Animation: Ubbe Iwerks, Rollin "Ham" Hamilton, Hugh Harman, Rudolph Ising. Ink and paint: Irene Hamilton, Walker Harman. Camera: Rudolph Ising.

Margie Gay (Alice).

Comic frenzy as a city hotel burns; Alice rides with fire chief to the rescue, followed by Julius driving a hook and ladder. Comic rescues of assorted animal residents. Julius sees lady cat stranded at top window, commandeers a black smoke cloud, and rides it up to save her.

Print source/s: AMS 35mm (as ALICE EN DE BRANDWEER).

ALICE CUTS THE ICE

Produced by Winkler Pictures Inc; distributed by FBO. In production May 1926. Negative cost: $1,156.74. Los Angeles preview at Bard's Hollywood Theater 5 June 1926. Copyright

Alice in the Wooly West; below, *Alice the Fire Fighter*. (Courtesy Nederlands Filmmuseum)

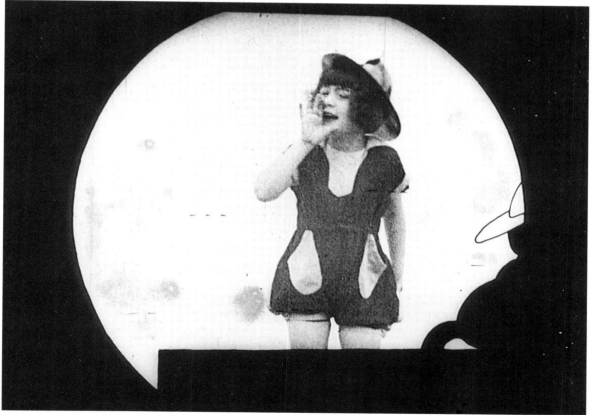

Alice Helps the Romance; below, *Alice's Rodeo*. (Courtesy Nederlands Filmmuseum)

R-C Pictures Corp 1 November 1926 LP23308. Release: 1 November 1926.
　　Animation: Ubbe Iwerks, Rollin "Ham" Hamilton, Hugh Harman, Rudolph Ising. Ink and paint: Irene Hamilton, Walker Harman. Camera: Rudolph Ising.
　　Margie Gay (Alice).
　　Julius the ice man elopes with Alice's maid in his ice wagon drawn by a drunken horse. Alice calls the cop on the beat and gives chase, but she arrives too late at the Justice of the Peace.

ALICE HELPS THE ROMANCE
Produced by Winkler Pictures Inc; distributed by FBO. In production May 1926; shipped 21 June 1926. Copyright R-C Pictures Corp 15 November 1926 LP23512. Release: 15 November 1926.
　　Animation: Ubbe Iwerks, Rollin "Ham" Hamilton, Hugh Harman, Rudolph Ising. Ink and paint: Irene Hamilton, Walker Harman. Camera: Rudolph Ising.
　　Margie Gay (Alice).
　　Julius loses his sweetheart to a rich, unscrupulous rival. Disconsolate, he decides to kill himself. Each suicide scheme fails; Alice finally saves him, and schemes to bring the sweetheart back to Julius. She arranges for two rough-neck cats to call Julius' rival their papa. The sweetheart, believing the rival a married father, returns to Julius.
　　Print source/s: AMS 35mm (as ROMANTIEK).

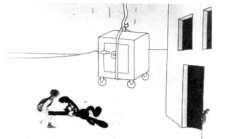

Alice Helps the Romance.
(Courtesy Nederlands Filmmuseum)

ALICE'S SPANISH GUITAR
Produced by Winkler Pictures Inc; distributed by FBO. In production May-June 1926; shipped 12 July 1926. Negative cost: $1,092.33. Copyright R-C Pictures Corp 29 November 1926 LP23614. Release: 29 November 1926.
　　Animation: Ubbe Iwerks, Rollin "Ham" Hamilton, Hugh Harman, Rudolph Ising. Ink and paint: Irene Hamilton, Walker Harman. Camera: Rudolph Ising.
　　Margie Gay (Alice).
　　Alice the Señorita plays guitar in a Spanish cafe; an infatuated Putrid Pete kidnaps her and takes her to his castle tower. Gaucho Julius, master of the whip, duels Pete and effects a leaping rescue a la Douglas Fairbanks.

ALICE'S BROWN DERBY
Produced by Winkler Pictures Inc; distributed by FBO. In production July 1926. Negative cost: $1,094.60. Los Angeles preview at Bard's Hollywood Theater 29 July 1926. Shipped 31 July 1926. Copyright R-C Pictures Corp 13 December 1926 LP23655. Release: 13 December 1926.
　　Animation: Ubbe Iwerks, Rollin "Ham" Hamilton, Hugh Harman, Rudolph Ising. Ink and paint: Irene Hamilton, Walker Harman. Camera: Rudolph Ising.
　　Margie Gay (Alice).
　　Horse trainer Alice has entered Julius as a jockey riding a mechanical horse in a local derby. Although Julius quickly takes the lead, his arch-rival the Bear changes road signs so that Julius nearly falls off a cliff. Halfway down the cliff, Julius fights off an eagle, commandeers its feathers, and rides a flying horse to the finish line.
　　Print source/s: AMS 35mm (as ALICE EN HET WONDERPAARD).

Alice's Brown Derby.
(Courtesy Nederlands Filmmuseum)

ALICE THE LUMBER JACK
Produced by Winkler Pictures Inc; distributed by FBO. In production July 1926; shipped 19 August 1926. Negative cost: $1,090.12. Copyright R-C Pictures Corp 27 December 1926 LP23616. Release: 27 December 1926.
　　Animation: Ubbe Iwerks, Rollin "Ham" Hamilton, Hugh Harman, Rudolph Ising. Ink and paint: Irene Hamilton, Walker Harman. Camera: Rudolph Ising.
　　Margie Gay (Alice).
　　Lumberjacks Alice and Julius caper as they fell trees and roll logs on the rapids; they are interrupted by the Bear and his rodent partner who seize Alice and hold her captive

in their canoe. Julius pursues them on a toboggan made from a dachshund.

ALICE THE GOLF BUG
Produced by Winkler Pictures Inc; distributed by FBO. In production July-August 1926; delivered 11 September 1926. Negative cost: $1,086.33. Copyright R-C Pictures Corp 10 January 1927 LP23592. Release: 10 January 1927.

Animation: Ubbe Iwerks, Rollin "Ham" Hamilton, Hugh Harman, Rudolph Ising. Ink and paint: Irene Hamilton, Walker Harman. Camera: Rudolph Ising.

Margie Gay (Alice).

Alice, Julius, and the Bear compete with other animals in a golf tournament. Julius, using his tail as a golf club, wins the cup accidentally when he squeezes an ostrich's neck to liberate his swallowed ball.

ALICE FOILS THE PIRATES
Produced by Winkler Pictures Inc; distributed by FBO. In production August 1926 as "Alice's Pirate Tale;" delivered 30 September 1926. Negative cost: $1,394.30. Copyright R-C Pictures Corp 24 January 1927 LP23877.

Animation: Ubbe Iwerks, Rollin "Ham" Hamilton, Hugh Harman, Rudolph Ising. Ink and paint: Irene Hamilton, Walker Harman. Camera: Rudolph Ising.

Margie Gay (Alice).

Julius is accidentally brought to a pirate ship commanded by Pete, and discovers Alice is held prisoner. He kills Pete's entire crew single-handed, duels Pete a la Fairbanks, and rescues Alice.

CLARA CLEANS HER TEETH (special production)
Produced by Walt Disney Studio for Dr. Thomas B. McCrum. In production late August 1926. Not copyrighted; no theatrical release.

Director: Walt Disney. Story: Margaret E. Greenwood, Eleanor M. Fonda. Animation: Ubbe Iwerks.

Marjorie Sewell (Clara), Lillian Worth (mother), George Morrell (father), Peggy the German shepherd.

Clara is so careless about dental health that she doesn't even seem to know what a toothbrush is. Prompted by the taunts of her classmates (who call her "Snaggle Tooth Susan") and an animated nightmare, she learns to take care of her teeth.

Print source/s: WDA 35mm.

ALICE AT THE CARNIVAL
Produced by Winkler Pictures Inc; distributed by FBO. In production August-September 1926; delivered 26 October 1926. Negative cost: $1,048.54. Copyright R-C Pictures Corp 7 February 1927 LP23901. Release: 7 February 1927. NYC premiere at Paramount Theater 20 February 1927 with *Love's Greatest Mistake* (Paramount).

Animation: Ubbe Iwerks, Rollin "Ham" Hamilton, Hugh Harman, Rudolph Ising. Ink and paint: Irene Hamilton, Walker Harman. Camera: Rudolph Ising.

Margie Gay (Alice).

Alice and Julius visit the carnival, see side show exhibits, and take comic rides on several attractions. Finally they ride a scenic railway and explode when they collide with another car.

ALICE'S RODEO (aka ALICE AT THE RODEO)
Produced by Winkler Pictures Inc; distributed by FBO. In production September 1926 as "Rodeo Story;" delivered 15 November 1926. Negative cost: $1,044.07. Copyright R-C Pictures Corp 21 February 1927 LP23873. Release: 21 February 1927.

Animation: Ubbe Iwerks, Rollin "Ham" Hamilton, Hugh Harman, Robert Edmunds, Rudolph Ising. Ink and paint: Irene Hamilton, Walker Harman. Camera: Rudolph Ising.

Margie Gay (Alice).

Alice's Rodeo.
(Courtesy Nederlands Filmmuseum)

Alice enters Julius in the bucking broncho contest; Julius wins, but the prize money is stolen by the Bear. Julius pursues the Bear on a saw horse, fights him hand-to-hand, and retrieves his money.

In both the original script and the copyright registration, the title is given as *Alice's Rodeo*.

Print source/s: AMS 35mm (as ALICE OP DE RODEO).

ALICE THE COLLEGIATE
Produced by Winkler Pictures Inc; distributed by FBO. In production October 1926; shipped 29 November 1926. Negative cost: $1,124.69. Copyright R-C Pictures Corp 7 March 1927 LP23881. Release: 7 March 1927.

Animation: Ubbe Iwerks, Rollin "Ham" Hamilton, Hugh Harman, Robert Edmunds, Rudolph Ising. Ink and paint: Irene Hamilton, Walker Harman. Camera: Rudolph Ising.
Margie Gay (Alice).

Football coach Alice watches Julius, her star quarterback, lead his team to victory. Comic plays include a dachshund stretching himself across the field to trip the other team and then shaping himself into a bicycle that Julius uses to ride over the goal line.

ALICE IN THE ALPS
Produced by Winkler Pictures Inc; distributed by FBO. In production October-November 1926; shipped 13 December 1926. Negative cost: $1,146.55. Copyright R-C Pictures Corp 21 March 1927 LP24213. Release: 21 March 1927.

Animation: Ubbe Iwerks, Rollin "Ham" Hamilton, Hugh Harman, Robert Edmunds, Rudolph Ising. Ink and paint: Irene Hamilton, Walker Harman. Camera: Rudolph Ising.
Margie Gay (Alice).

After assorted misadventures while skating with his friends in the Alps, Julius becomes a Swiss guide and takes the Bear hiking up an Alpine mountain.

ALICE'S AUTO RACE
Produced by Winkler Pictures Inc; distributed by FBO. In production November-December 1926; delivered 29 December 1926. Negative cost: $1,130.04. Copyright R-C Pictures Corp 4 April 1927 LP24363. Release 4 April 1927.

Animation: Ubbe Iwerks, Rollin "Ham" Hamilton, Hugh Harman, Robert Edmunds, Rudolph Ising, Paul Smith. Ink and paint: Irene Hamilton, Walker Harman. Camera: Mike Marcus.
Margie Gay (Alice: the last Margie Gay Alice).

Alice and Julius compete in an auto race. Despite a bad start and arch-rival Bear's switching road signs, Julius wins the race by bouncing his car over the heads of the other contestants.

ALICE'S CIRCUS DAZE

Alice's Circus Daze.
(Courtesy Nederlands Filmmuseum)

Produced by Winkler Pictures Inc; distributed by FBO. In production 31 December 1926 (live action) and January 1927 (animation) as "Circus Story;" delivered 31 January 1927. Negative cost: $1,176.09. Copyright R-C Pictures Corp 18 April 1927 LP24214. Release: 18 April 1927.

Animation: Ubbe Iwerks, Rollin "Ham" Hamilton, Hugh Harman, Paul Smith, Rudolph Ising. Ink and paint: Irene Hamilton, Walker Harman. Camera: Rudolph Ising.
Lois Hardwick (Alice).

Alice and Julius are circus acrobats, competing for the crowd's attention with a comic side show and a lion taming act. Up on the high wire, Julius balances Alice on a stack of chairs. Chairs collapse; Julius rescues the falling Alice with a tall step ladder.

Print source/s: WDA 35mm, LoC 35mm, AMS 35mm (as ALICE COMEDIE).

ALICE'S KNAUGHTY KNIGHT
Produced by Winkler Pictures Inc; distributed by FBO. In production 31 December

1926 (live action) and January 1927 (animation); delivered 17 January 1927. Negative cost: $1,162.80. Copyright R-C Pictures Corp 2 May 1927 LP24419. Release: 2 May 1927.

Animation: Ubbe Iwerks, Rollin "Ham" Hamilton, Hugh Harman, Paul Smith, Friz Freleng, Rudolph Ising. Ink and paint: Irene Hamilton, Walker Harman. Camera: Rudolph Ising.

Lois Hardwick (Alice).

In a big city tenement, Julius serenades his sweetheart, but is chased away by a bully rival in a suit of armor — Pete the Bear. Alice, a junk peddler, gives Julius the necessary supplies to fight back: a can opener with which to cut a hole in the armor, and a pot-bellied stove which he wears over himself.

ALICE'S THREE BAD EGGS

Produced by Winkler Pictures Inc; distributed by FBO. In production 31 December 1926 (live action) and February 1927 (animation); delivered 24 February 1927. Negative cost: $1,188. NYC debut at Paramount Theater 25 April 1927 with *Special Delivery* (Paramount). Copyright R-C Pictures Corp 16 May 1927 LP24555. Release: 16 May 1927.

Animation: Ubbe Iwerks, Rollin "Ham" Hamilton, Hugh Harman, Paul Smith, Friz Freleng, Ben Clopton, Norm Blackburn, Rudolph Ising. Camera: Rudolph Ising.

Lois Hardwick (Alice).

Alice and Julius command a fort in the pioneer west, drilling and inspecting the troops. When the fort is attacked by the Three Bad Eggs and their Indian cohorts, the duo command the resistance. They shoot cans of pepper at the marauders, repelling the attack.

ALICE'S PICNIC

Produced by Winkler Pictures Inc; distributed by FBO. In production January (live action) and March (animation) 1927; delivered 16 March 1927. Negative cost: $1,338.68. Copyright R-C Pictures Corp 30 May 1927 LP24580. Release: 30 May 1927.

Animation: Ubbe Iwerks, Rollin "Ham" Hamilton, Hugh Harman, Friz Freleng, Ben

Alice's Three Bad Eggs.
(Courtesy Walt Disney Company)

Clopton, Norm Blackburn, Les Clark, Rudolph Ising. Camera: Rudolph Ising.

Lois Hardwick (Alice).

Alice and her pals are out to enjoy a picnic: comic couples and families make their preparations and pour into their cars. Julius, his wife, and children bicycle to the grounds and join in assorted games. A gang of rats steal their food; Alice alerts the picnickers and leads the counter-attack.

ALICE'S CHANNEL SWIM

Produced by Winkler Pictures Inc; distributed by FBO. In production March 1927 (live action 26 March 1927). Negative cost: $1,385.52. NYC premiere at Paramount Theater 30 May 1927 with *A Million Bid* (Warner Bros.). Copyright R-C Pictures Corp 13 June 1927 LP24394. Release: 13 June 1927.

Animation: Ubbe Iwerks, Hugh Harman, Friz Freleng, Ben Clopton, Norm Blackburn, Les Clark, Rudolph Ising. Camera: Rudolph Ising.

Lois Hardwick (Alice).

Julius and Pete the Bear compete in an English Channel swimming competition, refereed by Alice. Bear fights dirty, finally knocking Julius cold. Down at the bottom of the channel, Julius is pursued by a shark and, in his frenzy, outswims everyone else.

ALICE IN THE KLONDIKE

Produced by Winkler Pictures Inc; distributed by FBO. In production ca. 31 January (live action) and February (animation) 1927; shipped 21 February 1927. Negative cost: $1,164.12. Copyright R-C Pictures Corp 27 June 1927 LP24239. Release: 27 June 1927. 529 ft.

Animation: Ubbe Iwerks, Rollin "Ham" Hamilton, Hugh Harman, Friz Freleng, Ben Clopton, Norm Blackburn, Rudolph Ising. Camera: Rudolph Ising.

Lois Hardwick (Alice).

Alice and Julius, gold rush prospectors in the Klondike, are enjoying themselves in a local dance hall when they hear they may have struck gold. Pegleg Pete the Bear steals the gold, but Julius runs after him, traps Pete in a hole, and takes the gold back.

Mintz confers with Disney in LA in March 1927; Universal commits to the Oswald series. Disney starts animating Oswald while finishing his last few Alices in March–early April 1927.

ALICE'S MEDICINE SHOW

Produced by Winkler Pictures Inc; distributed by FBO. In production ca. 26 March (live action) and April (animation) 1927; delivered 30 April 1927. Negative cost: $1,389. Copyright R-C Pictures Corp 11 July 1927 LP24395. Release: 11 July 1927.

Animation: Ubbe Iwerks, Hugh Harman, Friz Freleng, Paul Smith, Ben Clopton, Norm Blackburn, Les Clark, Rudolph Ising. Camera: Rudolph Ising.

Lois Hardwick (Alice).

Alice and Julius shill as barkers in a traveling medicine show. They demonstrate their patent medicine on a baldheaded elephant, a flea-ridden monkey, and a junkyard goat — with remarkable results. They chase two little pigs after watching them drinking from their bottles and getting drunk.

ALICE THE WHALER

Produced by Winkler Pictures Inc; distributed by FBO. In production March 1927 (live action ca. 26 March 1927). Negative cost: $1,339. NYC premiere at Paramount Theater 18 July 1927 with *Rolled Stockings* (Paramount). Copyright R-C Pictures Corp 25 July 1927 LP24383. Release: 25 July 1927.

Animation: Ubbe Iwerks, Hugh Harman, Friz Freleng, Ben Clopton, Norm Blackburn, Les Clark, Rudolph Ising. Camera: Rudolph Ising or Mike Marcus.

Lois Hardwick (Alice).

Alice the Whaler.

Alice and her crew dance and play on a deck of a whaling ship. The whaler's temperamental chef, a cat preparing food in the galley, demands eggs from his harried rodent assistant. The mouse shimmies up the foremast, captures a seagull, and extract three eggs. Julius sights a whale at play with its children. The monkey harpooner harpoons her, but the whale is so large that it swims out to sea, dragging the ship behind.

Print source/s: WDA 35mm (RKO reissue), UCLA 35mm (RKO reissue), FPA 35mm, CDF 35mm; GLASS 16mm, private collection 16mm.

ALICE THE BEACH NUT

Produced by Winkler Pictures Inc; distributed by FBO. In production ca. 26 March (live action) and April (animation) 1927. Los Angeles preview 14 June 1927. Negative cost: $1,334. Copyright R-C Pictures Corp 8 August 1927 LP24590. Release: 8 August 1927.

Animators: Ubbe Iwerks, Friz Freleng, Hugh Harman, Ben Clopton, Norm Blackburn, Les Clark. Camera: Mike Marcus.

Lois Hardwick (Alice).

Julius the lifeguard accompanies Alice to the beach. When a flirtatious society cat is carried out on a wave, Julius engineers her rescue: he gets rats to stretch a dachshund's body like a slingshot, has himself fired over the drowning girl, pulls out a rope ladder and drops it to her.

ALICE IN THE BIG LEAGUE

Produced by Winkler Pictures Inc; distributed by FBO. In production ca. 26 March (live action) and April (animation) 1927. Los Angeles preview 16 July 1927. Negative cost: $1,560. Copyright R-C Pictures Corp 22 August 1927 LP24553. Release: 22 August 1927.

Animation: Ubbe Iwerks, Friz Freleng, Hugh Harman, Rollin "Ham" Hamilton, Ben Clopton, Norm Blackburn, Les Clark. Camera: Rudolph Ising or Mike Marcus.

Lois Hardwick (Alice).

Alice umpires a baseball game as kids try to watch through a knothole. Among the comic plays, a hippo batter uses a telephone pole to swat the ball, a puppy outfielder chases the ball from the rear of a hook and ladder fire truck, and a runner slides into home plate on skates. Umpire Alice's bad calls lead to a general riot.

Print source/s: AMS 35mm (as ALICE SPEELT BASE-BAL).

Alice in the Big League.
(Courtesy Nederlands Filmmuseum)

"OSWALD THE LUCKY RABBIT"

POOR PAPA

A Winkler Production; distributed by Universal Pictures Corp. Shipped ca. 10 April 1927. Copyrighted by Universal Pictures 22 May 1928 LP25296. Release: 6 August 1928.*

Animation: Ubbe Iwerks, Hugh Harman, Friz Freleng, Rollin "Ham" Hamilton, Ben Clopton, Norm Blackburn, Les Clark, Rudolph Ising. Camera: Rudolph Ising.

Oswald declares war against storks who keep sending him baby rabbits. He tries to shoot them out of the sky; the storks, treating the babies like bombs, drop them down Oswald's chimney, lob them through his windows, and deliver them through sink faucets.

Trolley Troubles.

TROLLEY TROUBLES

A Winkler Production; distributed by Universal Pictures Corp. Shipped ca. 1 May 1927. Copyrighted by Universal Pictures 9 June 1927 LP24088. LA premiere at Criterion Theatre with *Flesh and the Devil* (MGM) 4 July 1927. NYC premiere at Roxy Theatre with *Singed* (Fox) 15 July 1927. Release: 5 September 1927. Reissued with added soundtrack 23 November 1931.

Animation: Ubbe Iwerks, Hugh Harman, Rollin "Ham" Hamilton, Friz Freleng, Ben Clopton, Norm Blackburn, Les Clark. Camera: Mike Marcus.

Lobby card for *Trolley Troubles*.
(Courtesy Walt Disney Company)

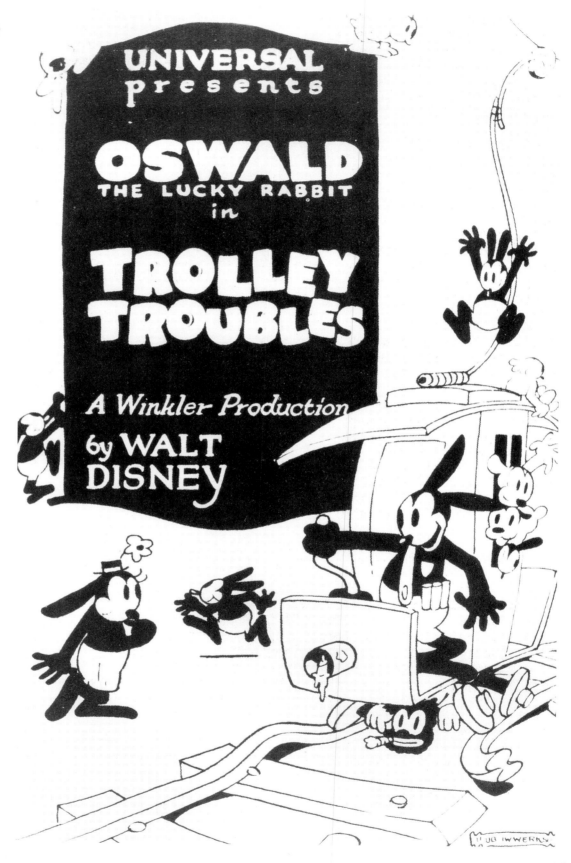

Oswald is the driver of a Toonerville trolley. Kids pester him for free rides, a cow causes trouble on the tracks, and the steep hills turn the excursion into a roller coaster ride.
Print source/s: WDA 35mm, UNIV 35mm.

OH TEACHER
A Winkler Production; distributed by Universal Pictures Corp. Copyrighted by Universal Pictures 20 July 1927 LP24227. Release: 19 September 1927. Reissued with added soundtrack 1 February 1932.
Animation: Ubbe Iwerks, Hugh Harman, Rollin "Ham" Hamilton, Friz Freleng, Ben Clopton, Norm Blackburn, Les Clark. Camera: Mike Marcus.
Schoolboy Oswald rides his girlfriend to school on his bicycle when a bully cat steals both the bike and sweetheart. During school recess, Oswald fights the bully, accidentally knocks him out, and reclaims his sweetheart.
Print source/s: WDA 35mm, UNIV 35mm.

GREAT GUNS
A Winkler Production; distributed by Universal Pictures Corp. Copyrighted by Universal Pictures 15 September 1927 MP4316. NYC premiere at Colony Theater with *Surrender* (Universal) on 10 October 1927. Release: 17 October 1927. Reissued with added soundtrack 29 February 1932.
Animation: Ubbe Iwerks, Hugh Harman, Rollin "Ham" Hamilton, Paul Smith, Friz Freleng, Ben Clopton, Norm Blackburn, Les Clark. Camera: Mike Marcus.
War is declared: Oswald enlists in the army and fights in the trenches. After a series of comic battles, he is blown to bits and reassembled by his girlfriend, who has become a Red Cross nurse.
Print source/s: WDA 35mm; GLASS 16mm, FPA 16mm, CDF 16mm.

THE MECHANICAL COW
A Winkler Production; distributed by Universal Pictures Corp. Copyrighted by Universal Pictures 10 September 1927 MP4314. Release: 3 October 1927. Reissued with added soundtrack 4 January 1932.
Animation: Ubbe Iwerks, Hugh Harman, Rollin "Ham" Hamilton, Paul Smith, Friz Freleng, Ben Clopton, Norm Blackburn, Les Clark. Camera: Mike Marcus.
Oswald the milkman has invented a robot-helper in the form of a cow. He sets up a milk stand, and customers fill their children with milk as though they were at a gasoline filling station. While Oswald moons with his girlfriend, a villain steals her away from him. Oswald and his Cow give chase.
Print source/s: WDA 35mm, UNIV 35mm; GLASS 16mm, FPA 16mm, CDF 16mm.

The Mechanical Cow.
(Courtesy Carlo Montanaro)

ALL WET
A Winkler Production; distributed by Universal Pictures Corp. Copyrighted by Universal Pictures 10 September 1927 MP4315. Release: 31 October 1927.
Story: Ubbe Iwerks (working title: "Ubbe's Beach Story"). Animation: Ubbe Iwerks, Hugh Harman, Rollin "Ham" Hamilton, Paul Smith, Friz Freleng, Ben Clopton, Norm Blackburn, Les Clark. Camera: Mike Marcus.
Oswald runs a Coney Island hot dog stand near the beach. He pursues the aloof Miss Rabbit, taking the place of a local life guard to watch her. Miss Rabbit, in turn, fakes a boating accident, hoping Oswald will rescue her. A large fish nearly turns Miss Rabbit's joke to disaster.
Print source/s: UNIV 35mm.

Note: For the remaining Oswald films we are unable to establish detailed animation credits. In July 1927, Disney split his animators into two units, one headed by Ubbe Iwerks and Friz Freleng, and the other by Hugh Harman and Ham Hamilton. Each team was provided additional animators, but it is usually impossible to know who was assigned to whom. We have assigned credits only when individual names could be specifically confirmed.

The animation pool at the time of the Iwerks-Freleng and Harman-Hamilton units consisted of Paul Smith, Ben Clopton, Norm Blackburn, Les Clark, and Johnny Cannon. Wilfred Jackson joined the company in April 1928.

THE OCEAN HOP

A Winkler Production; distributed by Universal Pictures Corp. Scenario started 11 July 1927; animation started 15 July 1927. Copyrighted by Universal Pictures 8 September 1927 LP24391. NYC premiere at Colony Theater 26 September 1927 with *Out All Night* (Universal). Release: 14 November 1927.

Animation: Hugh Harman, Rollin "Ham" Hamilton. Camera: Mike Marcus.

Oswald the amateur pilot enters a trans-Atlantic race, only to find his plane sabotaged by arch-rival Pete. Other planes compete, but Oswald wins by fashioning a superflier out of a dachshund.

Print source/s: WDA 35mm, UNIV 35mm; GLASS 16mm, FPA 16mm, CDF 16mm.

THE BANKER'S DAUGHTER

A Winkler Production; distributed by Universal Pictures Corp. Finished 12 August 1927; shipped 20 August 1927. Copyrighted by Universal Pictures 15 September 1927 MP4313. Release: 28 November 1927.

Story and animation: Ubbe Iwerks, Friz Freleng. Camera: Mike Marcus.

Oswald, limousine driver for a wealthy banker, is fired for flirting with the boss' daughter. When a gang led by Peg Leg Pete robs the boss' ritzy bank, Oswald gives chase, recovers the money, and wins Miss Cottontail.

HAREM SCAREM

A Winkler Production; distributed by Universal Pictures Corp. NYC premiere at Colony Theater 5 December 1927 with *Cheating Cheaters* (Universal). Copyrighted by Universal Pictures 20 December 1927 LP24785. Release: 9 January 1928.

Animation: Hugh Harman, Rollin "Ham" Hamilton. Camera: Mike Marcus.

Arabian desert adventure, with Oswald a tourist in a Moroccan cafe. Oswald falls in love with an Arabian dancing girl, but she is carried off by Pete the sheik. Oswald rides to the rescue on his drunken camel.

RICKETY GIN

A Winkler Production; distributed by Universal Pictures Corp. Working titles: "Whose Hootch," "Officer 999." Finished 2 September 1927; shipped 17 September. Copyrighted by Universal Pictures 19 October 1927 LP24531. Release: 26 December 1927.

Animation: Ubbe Iwerks, Friz Freleng. Camera: Mike Marcus.

Oswald the cop, mounted on his wooden police horse, flirts with a nurse who wheels a baby carriage in the park. Wanting to be alone with the nurse, Oswald lets his horse mind the baby. Meanwhile Pete, head of a bootleg liquor gang, gets Oswald drunk and woos the nurse wearing Oswald's stolen uniform.

NECK 'N' NECK

A Winkler Production; distributed by Universal Pictures Corp. Working title: "The Buggy Ride." Finished 17 September 1927; shipped 1 October. Copyrighted by Universal Pictures 28 December 1927 LP24811. Release: 23 January 1928.

Animation: Hugh Harman, Rollin "Ham" Hamilton. Camera: Mike Marcus.

Oswald takes Miss Rabbit out for a comic drive in his jalopy. Pursued by a traffic cop, Oswald's speeding car smashes into a tree. Dazed but unhurt, an angry Miss Rabbit drives off in a toy kiddie car she has kept in her pocket.

EMPTY SOCKS

A Winkler Production; distributed by Universal Pictures Corp. Working title: "Xmas Story." Copyrighted by Universal Pictures 23 November 1927 LP24696. Release: 12 December 1927. NYC premiere at the Roxy Theatre 25 December 1927 with *Silk Legs* (Fox).

Animation: Ubbe Iwerks, Hugh Harman, Rollin "Ham" Hamilton. Camera: Mike Marcus.

Oswald plays Santa Claus at an orphan asylum, but when the orphans accidently set their house on fire, Oswald plays fire fighter too.

THE OLE' SWIMMIN' OLE

A Winkler Production; distributed by Universal Pictures Corp. Finished 22 October 1927; shipped 29 October. Copyrighted by Universal Pictures 17 January 1928 LP24888. Release: 6 February 1928.

Animation: Hugh Harman, Rollin "Ham" Hamilton. Camera: Mike Marcus.

Oswald and his pals cavort in a swimming hole: they use a mule's body as a water slide, take dives, and steal the sleeping sheriff's suspenders for a swing.

AFRICA BEFORE DARK

A Winkler Production; distributed by Universal Pictures Corp. Working title: "Africa After Dark." Finished (animation) 2 November 1927; shipped 12 November. Copyrighted by Universal Pictures 3 February 1928 LP24972. Release: 20 February 1928.

Animation: Ubbe Iwerks. Camera: Mike Marcus.

Oswald, a big game hunter in Africa, stalks a variety of wild animals. He runs into trouble with a pack of lions and outwits them by turning his elephant into an airplane.

RIVAL ROMEOS

A Winkler Production; distributed by Universal Pictures Corp. Finished (animation) 3 December 1927; shipped 10 December. Copyrighted by Universal Pictures 16 February 1928 LP24996. NYC premiere at Colony Theatre 26 February 1928 with *The Leopard Lady* (DeMille/Pathé). Release: 5 March 1928.

Animation: Ubbe Iwerks.

Poor-but-honest Oswald competes with High Hat Pete for the hand of Lady Love. Oswald in his jalopy races with Pete in his swank roadster to her door step. Winning the race, Oswald serenades Lady Love on the banjo. A goat eats Oswald's music, then his banjo. Oswald responds by pulling the goat's mouth open and cranking his tail like a hurdy-gurdy. The quarreling suitors both lose out to a goofy dog who shows up on a motorcycle.

Print source/s: WYATT 16mm.

BRIGHT LIGHTS

A Winkler Production; distributed by Universal Pictures Corp. Working title: "Back Stage." Finished 12 November 1927; shipped 26 November. Copyrighted by Universal Pictures 1 March 1928 LP25033. Release: 19 March 1928.

Animation: Hugh Harman, Rollin "Ham" Hamilton. Camera: Mike Marcus.

Stage Door Johnny Oswald sneaks backstage to pursue a Cat Town follies girl. Chased on stage, he hides in a box, only to discover that the box is a tiger cage. Oswald shrinks and slips through the cage bars, but the tiger shrinks too and gives chase. Lions join the tiger, pursuing Oswald into the audience; the theater empties.

Print source/s: WDA 35mm, LoC 35mm.

SAGEBRUSH SADIE

A Winkler Production; distributed by Universal Pictures Corp. Copyrighted by Universal Pictures 14 March 1928 LP25069. Release: 2 April 1928.

Opposite and following page: Story sketches for *Ozzie of the Mounted.* (Courtesy Walt Disney Company)

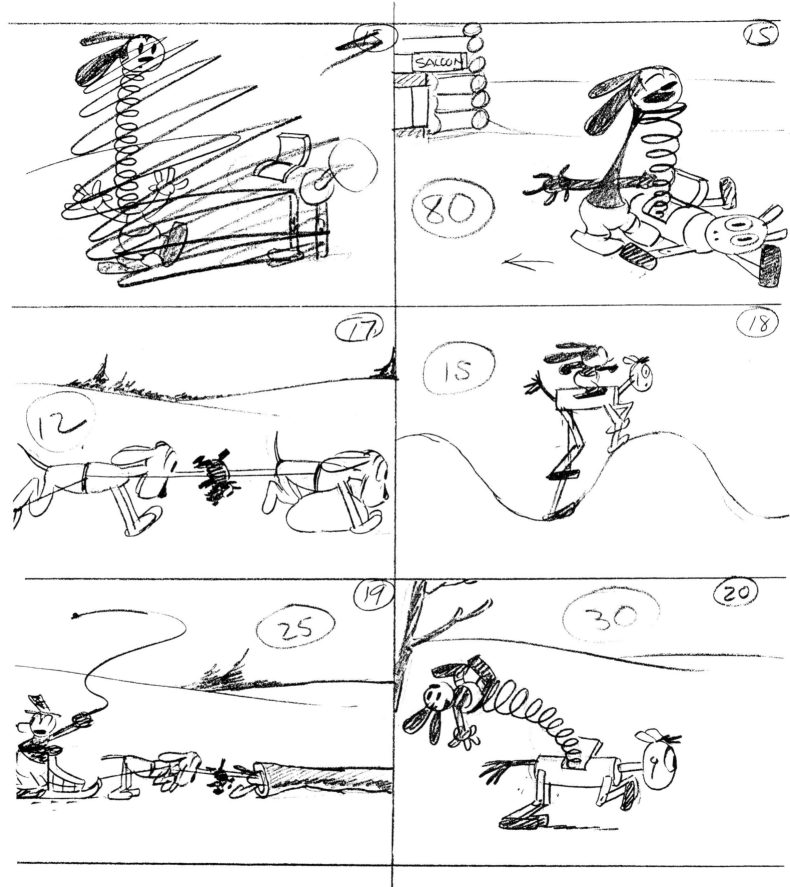

Animation: Ubbe Iwerks, Hugh Harman, Rollin "Ham" Hamilton. Camera: Mike Marcus.

Oswald the cowboy rescues Sadie on a runaway buckboard, with the villainous Peg Leg Pete in fast pursuit.

RIDE 'EM PLOWBOY!

A Winkler Production; distributed by Universal Pictures Corp. Working title: "An Ill Wind." Copyrighted by Universal Pictures 29 March 1928 LP25105. Release: 16 April 1928.

Animation: Ubbe Iwerks, Hugh Harman, Rollin "Ham" Hamilton, Friz Freleng. Camera: Mike Marcus.

Oswald the farmer works the comical, music-loving animals on his farm: he uses a pig for a plow, milks his cow to a musical beat, and gets a hen to lay her eggs in rhythm. A cyclone carries Oswald in the air; he saves himself by turning his cow into an airplane.

OZZIE OF THE MOUNTED

A Winkler Production; distributed by Universal Pictures Corp. Finished and shipped 25 January 1928. Copyrighted by Universal Pictures 29 March 1928 LP25106. Release: 30 April 1928. Total footage: 506 ft.

Animation: Ubbe Iwerks, Rollin "Ham" Hamilton, Hugh Harman, Ben Clopton, Les Clark. Camera: Mike Marcus.

An extended comic chase as Oswald the Mountie pursues murderer Foxy Wolf (alias Pegleg Pete, alias Putrid Pete) through the snow on an ill-functioning mechanical horse. Foxy Wolf escapes, but then tangles with a grizzly bear; in his frenzied escape, Foxy inadvertently runs into a jail cell.

HUNGRY HOBOES

A Winkler Production; distributed by Universal Pictures Corp. Working title: "Tramp Story." Copyrighted by Universal Pictures 30 March 1928 LP25129. Release: 14 May 1928.

Camera: Mike Marcus.

Oswald the hobo rides a freight train loaded with farm animals. He and his roughneck pal Putrid Pete use the tools at hand to cook themselves a meal. Discovered by a policeman, they are chased off the boxcar; they escape to a school yard. Pete fashions himself a hurdy-gurdy, turns a reluctant Oswald into a monkey, and entertains the children. The local sheriff chases them away.

OH, WHAT A KNIGHT

A Winkler Production; distributed by Universal Pictures Corp. Copyrighted by Universal Pictures 30 March 1928 LP25128. Release: 28 May 1928.*

Camera: Mike Marcus.

Oswald the medieval troubadour approaches a castle riding a mule. He serenades his sweetheart and, outwitting and outfighting her captor, Pete (in synopsis, the sweetheart's irate father), carries the damsel off with him.

Print source/s: WDA 35mm, LoC 35mm.

SKY SCRAPPERS

A Winkler Production; distributed by Universal Pictures Corp. Working title: "The Sky Scrapper." Finished and shipped 8 March 1928. Copyrighted by Universal Pictures 25 April 1928 LP25192. Release: 11 June 1928.*

Camera: Mike Marcus.

Oswald enjoys a lunch break on a skyscraper construction site. Fanny sells him a box lunch; his flirtation with her is interrupted by Pete, the surly foreman (called Wolf in the copyright synopsis). Pete spirits Fanny away with a grappling hook to a high steel girder, and Oswald climbs in pursuit.

Print source/s: WYATT 16mm.

THE FOX CHASE

A Winkler Production; distributed by Universal Pictures Corp. Copyrighted by Universal Pictures 6 June 1928 LP25345. Release: 25 June 1928.

Animation: Hugh Harman, Rollin "Ham" Hamilton. Camera: Mike Marcus.

Oswald the sportsman joins in a fox hunt, falling far behind because of an eccentric horse. Meanwhile, the resourceful fox has eluded his pursuers and outwitted a comic dachshund, but eventually finds himself trapped inside a hollow log. Oswald and his friends surround the log, but flee when a skunk emerges. Alone, the fox takes off his skunk disguise.

Print source/s: WYATT 16mm.

TALL TIMBER

A Winkler Production; distributed by Universal Pictures Corp. Working title: "Northwoods." Copyrighted by Universal Pictures 20 June 1928 LP25408. Release: 9 July 1928.

Animation: Hugh Harman, Rollin "Ham" Hamilton. Camera: Mike Marcus.

Oswald the outdoorsman canoes down the rapids, tries to hunt geese, shoots a hole in his canoe, and finds himself chased by the animals he has come to hunt. Chased into a bear cave, he emerges smartly attired in a bearskin coat and makes a quick getaway.

SLEIGH BELLS

A Winkler Production; distributed by Universal Pictures Corp. Copyrighted by Universal Pictures 3 July 1928 LP25444. Release: 23 July 1928.

Camera: Mike Marcus.

Oswald the winter sportsman plays in a fast hockey game, but is soon distracted by an aloof but beautiful skating rabbit. Helping her learn to skate, Oswald has her hold onto helium balloons. The balloons, however, send her into the sky; Oswald manages her aerial rescue.

The Fox Chase. (Courtesy Walt Disney Company)

HOT DOG

A Winkler Production; distributed by Universal Pictures Corp. Copyrighted by Universal Pictures 3 August 1928 LP25513. Release: 20 August 1928.

Camera: Mike Marcus.

Oswald the truant tries to sneak into a circus sideshow. After stealing a hot dog, he is pursued by the police, runs into a lion's cage, and escapes to another cage, only to discover he has hopped inside a patrol wagon.

"MICKEY MOUSE" (1928 productions)

PLANE CRAZY

Walt Disney Productions. In production April-May 1928. Los Angeles preview 15 May 1928. Soundtrack (music and effects) added ca. November 1928. NYC premiere at Mark Strand Theater 17 March 1929 with *Queen of the Night Clubs* (Warner Bros.). Copyrighted by Walter E. Disney. Silent version: 26 May 1928 MU5036. Sound version: 9 August 1930 MP1795.

Animation: Ubbe Iwerks. Ink and paint: Hazel Sewell, Lillian Disney, Edna Disney. Camera: Mike Marcus. Music: Carl Stalling.

Inspired by Charles Lindbergh, Mickey Mouse decides to build and fly his own airplane. His first attempt crashes before it ever gets off the ground, so he tries again, converting a jalopy into a plane. This effort works. Minnie Mouse goes along for the ride, but bails out when Mickey forces his attentions on her.

Print source/s: WDA 35mm, MoMA 35mm.

Plane Crazy.
(Copyright Walt Disney Company)

GALLOPIN' GAUCHO

Walt Disney Productions. In production June-August 1928 (interrupted by work on *Steamboat Willie*). Los Angeles preview 28 August 1928. Soundtrack (music and effects) added ca. November 1928. NYC premiere at Mark Strand Theater 30 December 1928 with *Scarlet Seas* (First National). Copyrighted by Walter E. Disney 9 August 1930 MP1794.

Animation: Ubbe Iwerks, Les Clark, Johnny Cannon, Wilfred Jackson. Music: Carl Stalling.

Mickey the gaucho stops for refreshment at a cantina where Minnie does a fiery dance. Their romance is cut short when Pete kidnaps Minnie. Mickey pursues them on his ostrich (who is now thoroughly drunk), defeats Pete in a Fairbanks-style duel, and rescues his sweetheart.

Print source/s: WDA 35mm, MoMA 35mm, LoC 35mm.

STEAMBOAT WILLIE

Walt Disney Productions. In production July-August 1928; sound recorded in New York September 1928. NYC premiere at Colony Theater 18 November 1928 with *Gang War* (FBO). Copyrighted by Walter E. Disney 21 November 1928 MP2124.

Animation: Ubbe Iwerks, Les Clark, Johnny Cannon, Wilfred Jackson. Music: Wilfred Jackson. Voices: Walt Disney (Mickey Mouse, parrot).

Mickey, the pilot of Pete steamboat, helps Minnie aboard when she arrives at the landing too late. Together, and with help from assorted animals on deck, they perform an unorthodox rendition of "Turkey in the Straw." But Pete is unimpressed with Mickey's musical prowess, and orders him to the galley to peel potatoes.

Print source/s: WDA 35mm, NFA 35mm, MoMA 35mm.

Key to Archival Sources

AMS	Nederlands Filmmuseum, Amsterdam
BAR	Filmoteca Generalitat de Catalunya, Barcelona
CDF	La Cineteca del Friuli, Gemona, Italy
DIF	Deutsches Institut für Filmkunde, Wiesbaden
FPA	Film Preservation Associates, Sun Valley, CA
GLASS	Murray Glass, EmGee Films, Encino, CA
HABER	Jerry Haber Collection, West Harford, Conn.
LoC	Library of Congress, Washington, D.C.
MoMA	The Museum of Modern Art, New York
MTL	La Cinémathèque Québécoise, Montreal
NFA	National Film Archive, London
NLM	National Library of Medicine, Bethesda, MD
PRA	Národní Filmový Archiv, Prague
UNIV	Universal Studio Vaults, Universal City, CA
WDA	Walt Disney Archive, Burbank, CA
WYATT	David Wyatt, London

BIBLIOGRAPHY

Barrier, Mike. "Silly Stuff: An Interview with Hugh Harman." *Graffiti* (Spring 1984), 6-11.

Barrier, Mike. "The Careers of Hugh Harman and Rudolf Ising." *Millimiter* (February 1976), 46-50.

Canemaker, John. *Felix*. New York: Pantheon Books, 1991.

Crafton, Donald. *Before Mickey*. Cambridge: MIT Press, 1982.

Klein, I. " 'Screen Gems' Made of Paste." *Funnyworld* 20 (Summer 1979), 39-41.

Lutz, E. G. *Animated Cartoons: How They Are Made, Their Origin and Development.* New York: Charles Scribner's Sons, 1925.

Merritt, Karen and Russell. "Mythic Mouse." *Griffithiana* 34 (December 1988), 58-71.

Paul, William. "Art, Music, Nature, and Walt Disney." *Movie* 24 (Summer 1970), 44-52.

Robinson, David. *Masterpieces of Animation 1833-1908.* Pordenone: Le Giornate del Cinema Muto, 1991, 8-19.

Thomas, Bob. *Walt Disney: An American Original.* New York: Simon and Schuster, 1976.

Thomas, Frank; Johnston, Ollie. *Disney Animation: The Illusion of Life.* New York: Abbeville, 1981.

Smith, David R. "Ub Iwerks, 1901-1971." *Funnyworld* 14 (Spring 1972), 32-37, 47.

Smith, David R. "Up to Date in Kansas City." *Funnyworld* 19 (Fall 1978), 22-34.

Smith, David R. "Disney Before Burbank." *Funnyworld* 20 (Summer 1979), 32-38.

Universal Weekly (June 1927-December 1928).

INDEX

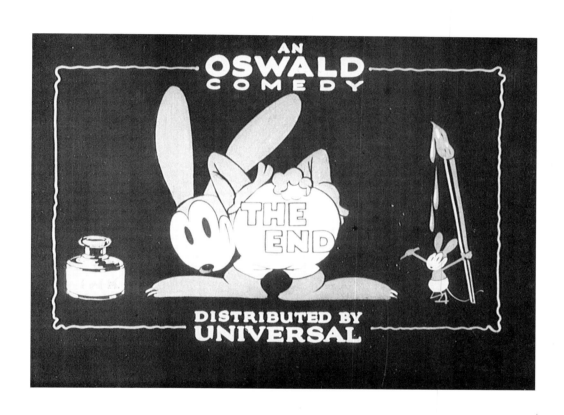

WALT IN WONDERLAND
THE SILENT FILMS OF WALT DISNEY

Typeset by
Desk Top Publishing Studio, Tricesimo

Printed by
Tipolitografia Sartor, Pordenone

Published by
Le Giornate del Cinema Muto
c/o La Cineteca del Friuli
Via Osoppo, 26
33013 Gemona (UD), Italy